Bianchi · Bliemel · Fitzpatrick · Quetz

Englisch für Erwachsene

Ausgabe B

Lehrbuch

Cornelsen & Oxford University Press

Verfasser Mary Bianchi, B.A. Düsseldorf; Realschullehrer Willibald Bliemel, B.A., Gelnhausen; Anthony Fitzpatrick, B.A., M.A., Heusenstamm; Prof. Dr. Jürgen Quetz, Bad Homburg v. d. H.

Verlagsredaktion Dr. Rolf Schneider

Zeichnungen Barbara Nichtweiß, Darmstadt; Richard Appleby, Truro; John Raines, Falmouth; Dennis Mallet, Chesham Bois

Fotos Billett Potter, Oxford; Klaus Wagener, Berlin; Maria Müller-Holtz, Oberhambach

Layout Hartmut Herold

Zu diesem Lehrbuch *Englisch für Erwachsene* Ausgabe B Band 1 gehören außerdem: Handbuch für den Kursleiter · Arbeitsbuch · Testaufgaben · Text- und Übungstonbänder · Compact-Cassetten · Textheft zu den Compact-Cassetten · Listening Comprehension-Cassetten · Arbeitsfolien

Das Zeichen 1 (mit eingedruckter Ziffer) bedeutet, daß Sie auf den Cassetten für den Kursteilnehmer zu EfE 1 Ausgabe B zusätzliche Übungen, kurze Dialoge und die Texte der B-Abschnitte finden. Die Benutzung der Cassette zu Hause wird Ihnen helfen, den jeweiligen Stoff gründlicher zu erarbeiten.
Das Zeichen (ohne Ziffer) bedeutet, daß sich auf einer gesonderten, nur für den Kursleiter erhältlichen Cassette eine Hörverständnis-Übung befindet, die zu den im Lehrbuch abgedruckten Texten oder Bildern unvorbereitet abgespielt werden soll.
Das Zeichen ▶ D2 oder ▶ AB4 unter einer Übung weist Sie darauf hin, daß Sie im Anschluß an diese betreffende Übung die stofflich ähnliche Übung **D 2** im Lehrbuch bzw. die Übung **4** der jeweiligen Unit im Arbeitsbuch bearbeiten können.

1.Auflage – 10.Druck 1987

Bestellnummer 31314

Satz Adolph Fürst & Sohn, Berlin

Druck CVK-Druck, Berlin

Weiterverarbeitung Fritzsche/Ludwig, Berlin

ISBN 3-8109-3131-4

Vertrieb Cornelsen-Velhagen & Klasing Verlagsgesellschaft, Bielefeld

Inhaltsverzeichnis

1 Die Themenformulierung orientiert sich an den Themenkatalogen aus ‚Das VHS-Zertifikat Englisch‘ und ‚Grundbaustein zum VHS-Zertifikat Englisch‘ des Deutschen Volkshochschulverbandes.

Vorwort

Englisch für Erwachsene Ausgabe B ist ein Sprachkurs für Volkshochschulen und andere Einrichtungen der Erwachsenenbildung. Er besteht aus drei Bänden und Begleitmaterial und soll Sprachkenntnisse vermitteln, die dem Lernenden erlauben, sowohl bei einem Auslandsaufenthalt als auch im eigenen Land Englisch in allen wichtigen Situationen als internationale Verkehrssprache anwenden zu können. *Englisch für Erwachsene* ist ein Lehrwerk für Anfänger ohne Vorkenntnisse und folgt den Richtlinien des Deutschen Volkshochschulverbandes. Es bietet in den beiden ersten Bänden eine Einführung in die wichtigsten Satzbaumuster der englischen Sprache und vermittelt einen für Gespräche in Alltagssituationen wichtigen Grundwortschatz von ca. 1.300 Vokabeln.

Mit Hilfe dieses sprachlichen Wissens kann man eine Reihe von Sprechabsichten verwirklichen und sich in einer begrenzten Anzahl von Alltagssituationen über verschiedene Themen verständigen, wie dies in den Broschüren ‚Das VHS-Zertifikat Englisch'/ ‚Grundbaustein zum VHS-Zertifikat Englisch' dargestellt ist. Die hierfür notwendigen Fertigkeiten ‚Hörverstehen', ‚Sprechfertigkeit', ‚Leseverstehen' und bis zu einem gewissen Grad auch ‚Schriftlicher Ausdruck' können in einem Kurs mit *Englisch für Erwachsene* intensiv geübt werden.

Das Lehrwerk ist so angelegt, daß Erwachsene die fremde Sprache im lebendigen Gespräch miteinander lernen können. In vielen Fällen gehen unsere Übungen von den eigenen Erfahrungen der Lernenden aus, über die mit einfachsten sprachlichen Mitteln berichtet werden kann. Die Kursteilnehmer lernen, ihre Sprechabsichten in Gesprächen mit anderen Lernenden zu verwirklichen. Sie lernen die sprachliche Bewältigung von Alltagssituationen durch sprachliches Handeln und nicht durch Regelpauken und mechanische Grammatikübungen. Texte und Themen sind so ausgewählt, daß sie den Interessen Erwachsener entsprechen und zum Meinungsaustausch anregen. Von der ersten Sitzung an können die Lernenden kommunikativ sinnvolle Äußerungen machen.

Die Verweise (z. B. § 22) über den C-Teilen des Lehrbuchs beziehen sich auf einen oder mehrere Paragraphen in der *Englischen Grammatik für Erwachsene*, Bestellnummer 5259. Dort werden die im C-Teil des Lehrbuchs aufgeführten grammatischen Strukturen auf deutsch erläutert. Die *Englische Grammatik für Erwachsene* wurde für Anfänger mit englischen Vorkenntnissen geschrieben. Da in dieser Grammatik auch das System beschrieben wird, in das grammatische Einzelheiten eingebunden sind, gehen die Informationen oft über das hinaus, was Sie im Unterricht durchgenommen haben. Dies trifft besonders auf die Paragraphen der Grammatik zu, auf die in Klammern verwiesen wird.

Die Verfasser

Unit 0 **Hello, how are you?**

1

– What's	his her	name?	– His Her	name is	

– I'm . . . .

– Hello, ... My name is Tony. Nice to meet you.

– Nice to meet you, too.

► AB 3

1 2 Hello, how are you?

► AB 2, AB 4

3

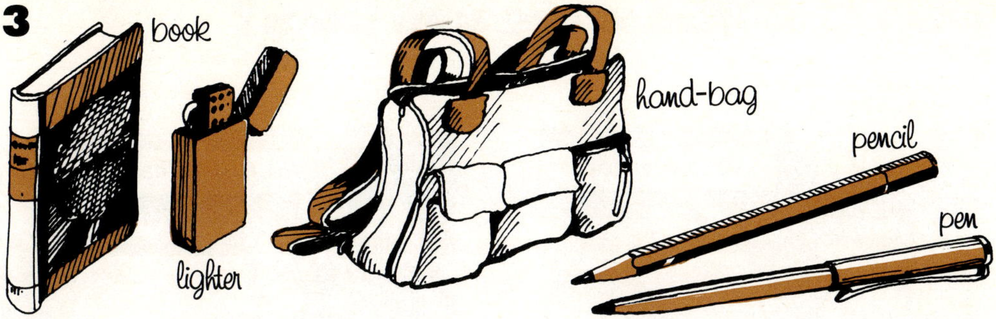

– Is this	your his her Helen's Peter's	pen? . . . ?

– Yes, it is.	
No, it isn't. It's	Peter's. Helen's. . . . .

► AB 1

4

'Is your name Peter Miller?'
'No. Why?'

'Because that is Peter Miller's coat.'
'Who is Peter Miller?'

'I am.'

Where are you from?

A1

– Is this your	pen? book? . . . ?	– Yes, it is. No, it isn't. That's my . . . .

► AB 3

A2

– Whose	pen hand-bag . . .	is this?

– It's	Jane's Jim's . . . my	pen. . . . .

► C 2

A3

– Who's that lady over there?
– That's not a lady.
That's my wife.

A 4 Where are you from?

– Where are you from?
  – I'm from . . . .

– Are you from . . . ?
  – No, I'm not. I'm from . . . .

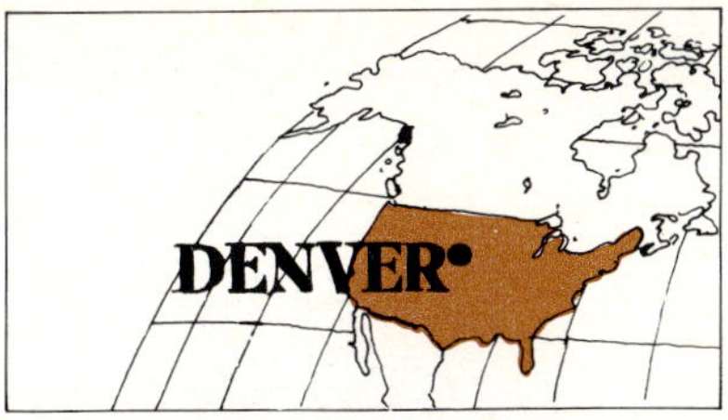

Denver is a city in America.

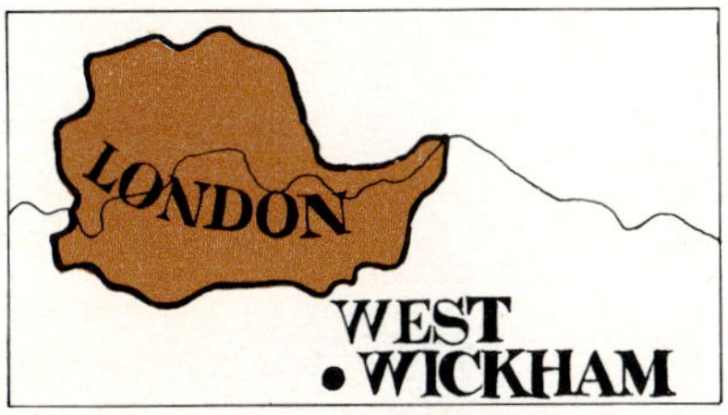

West Wickham is a village near London.

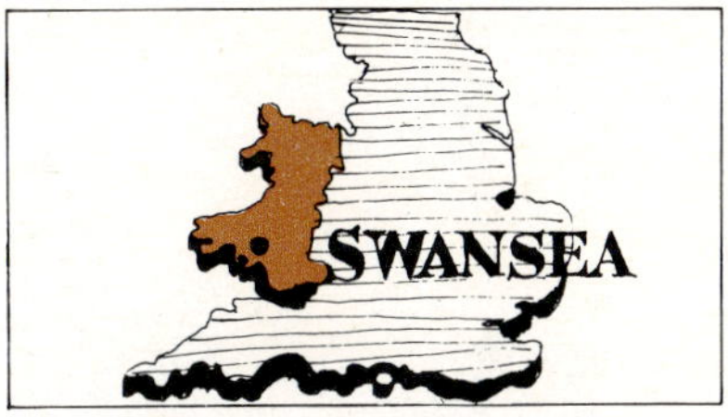

Swansea is a town in Wales.

A 5 Can you spell it, please?

Mr Richard Green
Bristol (England)

Miss Audrey Walker
Vancouver (Canada)

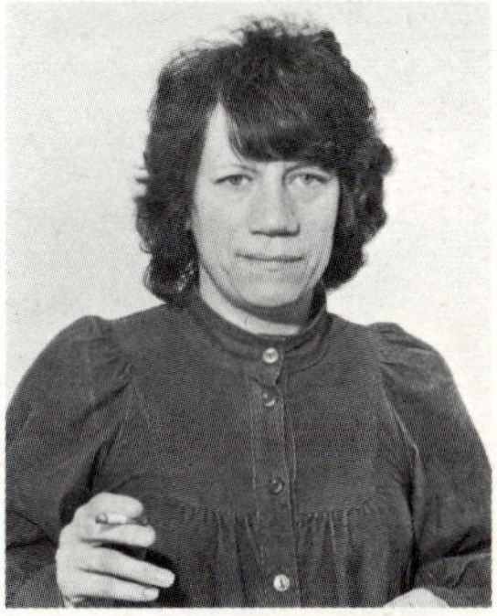

Mrs Mary J. Robinson
Denver (United States)

– Good evening. My name is Brown.
  – Good evening, Mr Brown. And what's your first name, please?
– Dick.
  – And where are you from, Mr Brown?
– Horsley.
  – Can you spell that, please?
– . . . .
  – Thank you. Here's your key.

A 6 This is . . .

– Andrew, this is Carl Wagner. He's from Germany. He's here on business. Carl, this is Andrew Harris.

– How do you do?

– How do you do? Where are you from in Germany, Mr Wagner?

– Pulling. It's a village near Munich.

– I'm from Boston.

– Yes, Andrew is ICC's sales manager here in England.

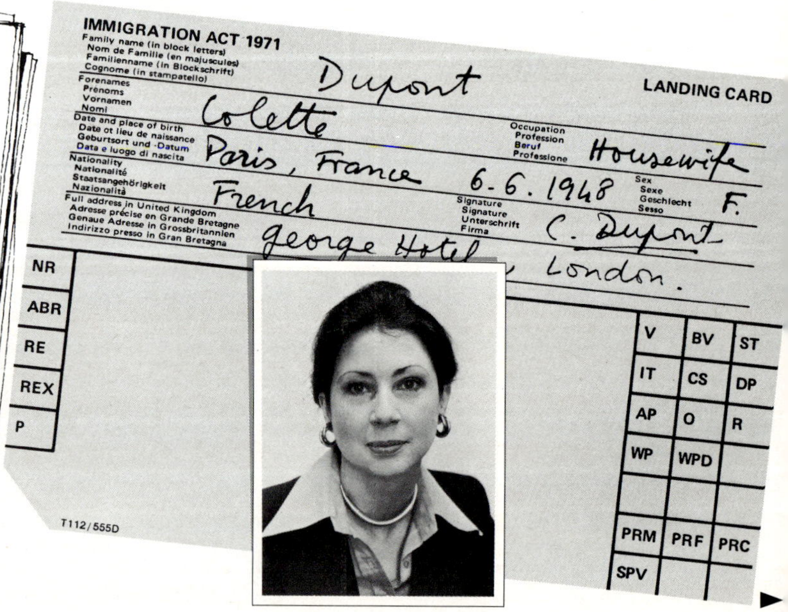
IMMIGRATION ACT 1971

LANDING CARD

Family name (in block letters) / Nom de Famille (en majuscules) / Familienname (in Blockschrift) / Cognome (in stampatello): Dupont

Forenames / Prénoms / Vornamen / Nomi: Colette

Date and place of birth / Date et lieu de naissance / Geburtsort und -Datum / Data e luogo di nascita: Paris, France 6.6.1948

Occupation / Profession / Beruf / Professione: Housewife

Nationality / Nationalité / Staatsangehörigkeit / Nazionalità: French

Sex / Sexe / Geschlecht / Sesso: F.

Signature / Signature / Unterschrift / Firma: C. Dupont

Full address in United Kingdom / Adresse précise en Grande Bretagne / Genaue Adresse in Grossbritannien / Indirizzo presso in Gran Bretagna: George Hotel, London.

NR ABR RE REX P

V BV ST IT CS DP AP O R WP WPD PRM PRF PRC SPV

T112/555D

►

– Where's	Patrick Mulligan . . .	from?		– He's She's	from	Ireland. . . . .

– What's	Carl Wagner's . . .	job?		– He's	a businessman. an actor. . . . .

– Where's	Pulling? . . . ?		– It's . . . .

– Who's that over there?

– It's	He's	a German businessman. an American . . . . an . . . .
	She's a French	

This is Patrick Mulligan's car.
It's a Mini.
It's an English car.
It's in front of the hotel.

– Where's Patrick Mulligan's car?	– It's . . . .
– Whose car is in front of the hotel?	– It's Patrick Mulligan's.

▸ D 4, D 5, AB 4, AB 5, AB 7

A 7

Listen, please

Who is it?

a

Graham Green,
from Birmingham.

b

Graham Greene,
from Liverpool.

c

Graham Grime,
from Liverpool.

3 **B**

IN A HOTEL IN LONDON

Carl Wagner – Is that Alex Dupont over there?

Andrew Harris – Yes, it is. But who's the lady?

Carl Wagner – Oh, I think she's his wife.

Mr Dupont – Hello, Carl. Nice to meet you again. Colette, this is Carl Wagner. He's a businessman from Germany. He's from Munich.

Carl Wagner – Well, I'm from a village near Munich. How do you do?

Colette Dupont – How do you do?

Mr Dupont – How are you, Carl?

Carl Wagner – Very well, thank you.

Mr Dupont – Is your wife with you?

Carl Wagner – No, she isn't, I'm afraid.

Mr Dupont – Oh, are you here on business?

Carl Wagner – Yes, I am. I'm here for the boat show. And you?

Colette Dupont – My husband is here on business, too.

Mr Dupont – Cigarette?

Carl Wagner – No, thank you.

Mr Dupont – Where's my lighter?

Colette Dupont – It's in my hand-bag, dear. Here you are.

Mr Dupont – Oh, thanks a lot.

Colette Dupont – Who's that man over there? Is it Richard Burton?

Carl Wagner – The man at the bar? Oh, no, that's Andrew Harris. He's a sales manager from Boston. He's here for the boat show, too.

Colette Dupont – No, not the man at the bar, the man at the reception.

Mr Dupont – That's not Richard Burton, dear. That man's car is in front of the hotel, and it's only a Mini, not a Rolls-Royce.

Carl Wagner – You're right, Alex. It's Patrick Mulligan. But he's an actor, too. He's an Irish actor.

▶ D 1, D 2, AB 1

C 1

a	lighter	an	actor
	book		English car
	town		Irish businessman
	...		o...
			u...

§ 123 ▶ D 3

C 2

 [z]	 [s]
This is Bob's car.	This is Philip's car.
Richard's	Pat's
Meg's	Dick's
Carl's	Elizabeth's
Jim's	
Helen's	
Peter's	
Joe's	
Nancy's	
Andrew's	
and: Andrew Harris's [sɪz] car	

§ 119

C 3

§ 151 ►D 6

C 4 to be

I	am	a sales manager.
You	are	right.
He	is	an Irish actor.
She	is	his wife.
It	is	Patrick Mulligan's car.

we write	*we say*
I am	I'm
you are	you're
he is	he's
she is	she's
it is	it's

His name is Smith. His name's Smith.

(§§ 28, 153) ►D 5

C 5 Yes/no-questions and short answers

– Are you from London?	– Yes, I am. No, I'm not.
– Is this your lighter?	– Yes, it is. No, it isn't.
– Is Patrick Mulligan an actor?	– Yes, he is.
– Is Mr Mulligan a businessman?	– No, he isn't.
– Am I right?	– Yes, you are. No, you aren't.

we write	*we say*
I am not	I'm not
you are not	you aren't
he is not	he isn't
she is not	she isn't
it is not	it isn't

§ 18 ►AB 8

C 6 W-questions

we write	*we say*
Who is this? Where is my lighter?	– Who's this? – Where's my lighter?
Where is he from? What is his job? Whose car is this?	– Where's he from? – What's his job?

WHO is this? WHERE is he from?

§§ (162, 163), 165, 168 ►D 4

C 7

§ 135 ►AB 3

C 8 ... too

He's an actor, too.
Nice to meet you, too.
I'm from London, too.
He's here on business, too.

§ 205 ►AB 11

D 1

Answer the questions:

1 Is Alex Dupont from Germany?
2 Is Colette Mr Dupont's wife?
3 Is Carl Wagner a businessman from Germany?
4 Is the lighter in Colette's hand-bag?
5 Is the man at the bar Richard Burton?
6 Is Patrick Mulligan's car in front of the hotel?
7 Is Patrick Mulligan a businessman from Germany?
8 Is Boston a village near Munich?
9 Is Andrew Harris a sales manager?

D 2 *Who says what? Mr Dupont, Carl Wagner or Colette Dupont?*

.... – Colette, this is Carl Wagner. He's a businessman from Germany.
.... – My husband is here on business, too.
.... – Is your wife with you?
.... – Who's that man over there? Is it Richard Burton?
.... – I'm from a village near Munich.
.... – It's in my hand-bag, dear.
.... – You're right, Alex. It's Patrick Mulligan.

D 3 A or an?

Patrick Mulligan is ... Irish actor.
Mr Green is ... English businessman.
Mr Harris is ... businessman.
He is .... American businessman.
Carl Wagner is ... German businessman.
Philip White is ... sales manager.
Cork is ... Irish town.
That's ... nice car.
Swansea is ... town near Bristol.

► AB 5

D 4 *Ask the questions:*

– Who's this?	– It's Mr Green.
– Where's ... ?	– He's from England.
– ... ?	– It's Patrick Mulligan.
– ... ?	– He's an Irish actor.
– ... ?	– It's Miss Walker.
– ... ?	– She's from Canada. And here's Mrs Robinson.
– ... ?	– She's from Denver. And here's Carl Wagner.
– ... ?	– He's a businessman. He's here with Mr Harris.
– ... ?	– He's from the United States, too.

► AB 4

D 5 I, you, he, she or it?

1 My name is Patrick Mulligan. ... 'm an actor.
2 His wife is from Ireland. ... 's at the reception.
3 Her hand-bag isn't here. ... 's in the car.
4 Alfred is a sales manager. ... 's from Munich.
5 I'm here on business. Are ... here on business, too?
6 Where's my lighter? ... isn't in my hand-bag.
7 How are ..., Carl? Is your wife with you?
8 How do ... do?

► AB 7

D 6 My, your, his or her?

1	– Is your wife with you?	– No, ... wife isn't here.
2	– Is this Colette's car?	– No, it isn't, ... car is in front of the hotel.
3	– Is this your pen?	– No, it isn't, ... pen is in the car.
4	– Is this Mary's pen?	– No, it isn't, ... pen is in her hand-bag.
5	– Is Andrew's lighter in the car?	– No, it isn't, ... lighter is in his wife's hand-bag.
6	– Is this your hand-bag?	– No, it isn't, ... hand-bag is in the car.
7	– Is that Carl's wife?	– No, it isn't, ... wife is at the reception.
8	– Mary, where is my lighter? Is it in your car?	– No, it isn't, ... lighter is in ... hand-bag.

► AB 6

Englisch hören, sprechen und lesen...
Zu Hause lernen bringt Sie voran

Erster Vorschlag:

Zwei Sprachcassetten und ein Textheft

In diesem Lehrbuch finden Sie neben einigen Übungen der **A**- und **D**-Teile sowie neben dem **B**-Text ein **Cassettensymbol** mit einer Nummer. Diese Nummer verweist auf eine Cassetten-Übung, mit deren Hilfe Sie den jeweiligen Stoff noch vertiefen können. Zu den **A**-Teilen gibt es auf den Cassetten „Mini-Dialoge" mit wichtigen Redewendungen. Sie üben hier zunächst die Rolle eines der beiden Sprecher ein. Dann können Sie diese selbst übernehmen und im Wechsel mit dem anderen Sprecher bis zur Geläufigkeit anwenden.

Bei den Grammatikübungen im Anschluß an Übungen der **D**-Teile im Lehrbuch handelt es sich ebenfalls um rollenspielartige Szenen. Wenn Sie die Rolle eines Sprechers übernehmen, bleiben Ihre Antworten im Rahmen eines grammatischen Musters.

Die Texte der Mini-Dialoge und der Sprechübungen sind in einem **Textheft** abgedruckt, in dem Sie sich über Art und Umfang der Übungen informieren können. Die **B**-Texte auf den Cassetten sind mit den im Lehrbuch abgedruckten Fassungen identisch.

Bitte beachten Sie auch die folgende Seite!

Bestellkarte

Hiermit bestelle ich die im Kästchen angekreuzten Arbeitsmittel zur Lieferung **gegen Nachnahme** direkt an umseitige Anschrift oder durch die nachstehend angegebene Buchhandlung.

____

____

☐ 2 **Sprachcassetten** zum Lehrbuch „Englisch für Erwachsene" 1 B
Gesamtlaufzeit ca. 120 Minuten. Unverbindliche Preisempfehlung 39,90 DM.
Bestellnummer 31357

☐ 1 **Textheft** der Sprechübungen auf den Sprachcassetten
24 Seiten, DIN A5, geheftet 4,80 DM. Bestellnummer 31349.

☐ 1 **Arbeitsbuch** zum Lehrbuch „Englisch für Erwachsene" 1 B
112 Seiten, kartoniert 13,60 DM. Bestellnummer 31322.

☐ 1 **Englische Grammatik für Erwachsene**
112 Seiten, zweifarbig, kartoniert 13,–– DM. Bestellnummer 5259.

☐ 1 **Reader "Have you got a minute?"**
56 Seiten, zweifarbig, kartoniert 8,35 DM. Bestellnummer 32370.

Stand der Preise vom 1. 1. 1987. Änderungen vorbehalten.

Name und Anschrift bitte umseitig eintragen!

Zweiter Vorschlag:

Arbeitsbuch zum Wiederholen

Das Arbeitsbuch zu „Englisch für Erwachsene“ 1B beginnt mit ausführlichen Ratschlägen zum Thema „Wie lerne ich zu Hause?“ und stellt dann zu jeder Unit des Lehrbuches sieben Arten von Übungen mit Lernhilfen bereit. So können Sie nachbereiten und vertiefen, was Sie sich im Kurs angeeignet haben.

Dritter Vorschlag:

Englische Grammatik für Erwachsene

Diese Grammatik von Prof. Dr. W. Hüllen wurde in enger Verbindung mit Ihrem Lehrbuch entwickelt. Eine besonders übersichtliche Gliederung des Stoffes hilft Ihnen, alle gewünschten grammatischen Informationen rasch zu finden. Beispielsätze in leicht verständlichem Englisch verdeutlichen die Regeln, die in deutscher Sprache angeboten werden. Dabei wird immer dort, wo es sinnvoll ist, zum Vergleich auf Erscheinungen der deutschen Sprache hingewiesen.

Vierter Vorschlag:

Leseheft “Have you got a minute?”

Schon mit geringen Vorkenntnissen können Sie dieses interessante und abwechslungsreich gestaltete Leseheft als häusliche Lektüre heranziehen. Es werden viele aktuelle Themen angesprochen, Informationen über Großbritannien gegeben und in bunter Folge Bildgeschichten, Spiele, Rätsel und Denksportaufgaben eingeschoben.

Versandanschrift

Name

Vorname

Straße/Hausnummer

PLZ

Ort

Best.-Dat.

PR-SU | RA | URA | SA | MA | Text | NBKZ | E

Postkarte

Bitte als Postkarte freimachen

Cornelsen-Velhagen & Klasing
Verlagsgesellschaft
Postfach 87 29

4800 Bielefeld 1

D 7 *Write what Richard Brown and John Miller say.*

1

Richard Brown ...
John Miller ...

2

John Miller ...
Richard Brown ...

3

Richard Brown ...

4

John Miller ...
Richard Brown ...

5

John Miller ...
Richard Brown ...

6

John Miller ...
Richard Brown ...

Unit 2

Rooms and houses

A 1 What's the number of your house?

► AB 4

A 2 There's only one

– What is there in Mr and Mrs Scott's living-room?

– There is	a an	desk. armchair. lamp. table. TV.
There are	two . . . a lot of	chairs. pictures. books on the shelf.

►

Miss Gardener's living-room

Mr and Mrs Black's living-room

– What is there in your living-room?
How many | chairs / ... | are there in your living-room?

– There is a . . . .
There are . . . .
There's only one.
There are none.

► AB 2, C 2

A 3 It's very comfortable

– This chair is (very) nice/comfortable/old.

– Yes,	very quite	nice, . . . ,	and it isn't very expensive. but it's very expensive.

► AB 7

1 A 4 How much is it?

– How much is the	lamp armchair TV table picture	on the left? on the right? in the middle?

– It's	a hundred and ninety pounds fifty.	
	ninety-nine . . .	pence. p.

► C 1

A 5

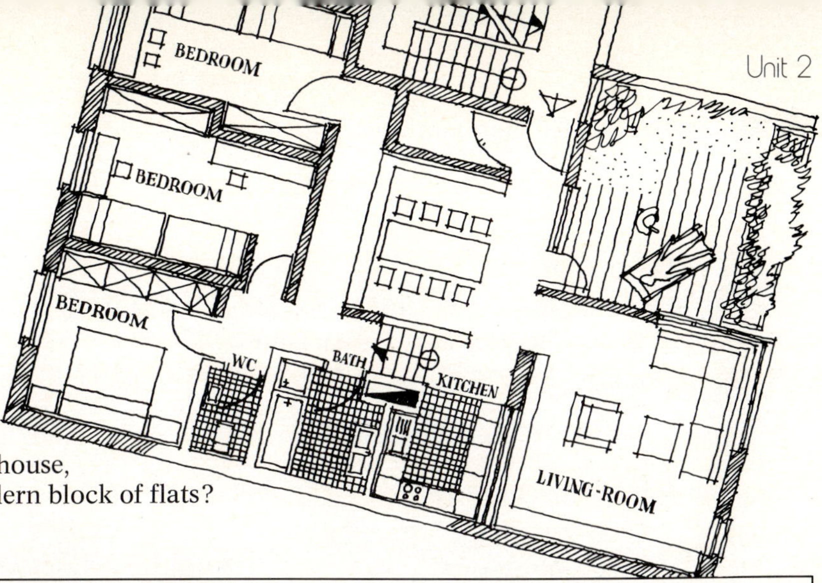

Is this a house,
a flat in an old house,
or is it in a modern block of flats?

Houses and flats

BLACKHEATH

3 bed. hse., living rm., kitchen, bath/wc, Gge. & gdn. with fine old trees. £135 per week. 850 6740

HOLLAND PARK W14

Basement flat, 2 rms., kitchen, £75 pw. 229 7870

CENTRAL LONDON

1, 2 and 3 bedrm. flats in mod. block in quiet street, from £75 to £225. John Richards & Co. 937 2561

gdn.	=	garden
Gge.	=	garage
bed./bedrm.	=	?
rm./rms.	=	?
hse.	=	?
mod.	=	?
pw.	=	?

A 6 – Can you tell me about where you live?

– I live in	a block of flats an old house	in . . . .

– Is it near here?

– Yes, it is. No, it isn't.	It's	. . . minutes an hour half an hour	from here	by	car. bus. Underground.
				on foot.	

– Is it in a quiet street?

– Yes, it is.
No, it isn't.

'Get out of my garden!'

– Is there a park near your house?

– Yes, there is.
No, there isn't.

– Is there a garden?

– Yes, ...
No, ...

– Are there a lot of	old trees flowers	in your garden?

– Yes, ...
No, ...

– How many rooms are there in your . . . ?

– There are . . . . There are . . . bedrooms, and there's a kitchen, a bathroom, a living-room, ...

– What can you see from your living-room window?

– You can see	a lot of houses. a park. . . . .

Now tell the class about where you live.

– I live in a . . . , . . . minutes from here. It's . . . . There's a . . . .
There are . . . .

► D 2, D 3

A 7 I think it's quite expensive

– Is the house in Blackheath expensive?
Is the flat near Holland Park expensive?
Are the flats in Central London expensive?

– Yes, I think it is.
Well, it's quite expensive.
Not really.
Oh, yes, very expensive.
Oh no, it's quite cheap.

Houses are not very expensive in England, but flats are.
And what about Germany?

– Well, houses are . . . , but flats aren't.

– Is your	house flat	expensive?

– . . . .

Sometimes it's difficult to find a cheap	flat. room. house.

– Is it difficult to find cheap	flats rooms houses	in	Fulda? Hamburg? . . . ?

– Yes, ...
. . . .

A 8 Listen, please

Is it this flat . . . or this house . . . or this house?

a
CENTRAL LONDON
3 bedroom flat
£120 per week

b
CENTRAL LONDON
4 bedroom house
£100 per week

c
CENTRAL LONDON
3 bedroom house
£100 per week

A 9 Listen, please

How much is this flat? It's . . . .

How many rooms are there? There are . . . .

2 B

ROOMS

- Hello, Jane.
- Hello, how are you?
- Fine. How's your new room?
- Oh, it's very nice, very comfortable, very quiet.
- Where is it?
- Near Regent's Park, in Chester Terrace, five minutes from the Zoo.
- Oh, can you *see* the Zoo from your room?
- No, but you can see the trees in the park, and sometimes you can *hear* the animals.
- Is it expensive?
- Oh, not really. It's very comfortable, you know. There are two very old armchairs in it, and there's a colour TV.
- How much is it?
- £20 a week. But it's very nice. Is your flat nice?
- It's only a room.
- Where is it?
- It's in an old house. In the basement. It's near Holland Park.
- Oh, can you see the park from your room?
- No.
- Well, what can you see?
- Hm, there's the entrance to the Underground. There are the cars and buses – there's a lot of traffic even at night.
- Is it expensive? How much is it?
- £25 a week.
- Yes, it's difficult for an African student to find a cheap room in London.

► D 1, AB 1, AB 5

C 1

A THE [ə]	AN THE [ɪ]
room tree hotel car name ...	actor entrance Irish actor old house Underground
	an/the [ɪ] → a, e, i, o, u

§§ 122, 123

C 2

two three four ...	books lamps [s] cigarettes	hand-bags jobs [z] husbands pens lighters ...	entrances buses [sɪz]

We write city – cities shelf – shelves	*We say* houses [zɪz]

§§ 107, (108–110)

C 3

There **is a** bathroom.	There **are two** bathrooms.

§ 20 ►D 2

C 4

Yes/no-questions and short answers

Is there **a** bathroom?	– Yes, there **is**. No, there isn't.
Are there **two** bathrooms?	– Yes, there **are**. No, there aren't.

§ 20 ►D 3

C 5 **W-questions**

What is there in your living-room? (§§ 137, 166) ►D 4, AB 2

How many books **are** there on the desk?	There **is** only **one**
How many flats **are** there in this block?	There **are 28**
How many animals **are** there in the zoo?	There **are a lot of** animal**s** in the zoo.
but: **How much is this** book?	It's £3.10.

C 6

1	one [wʌn]	11	eleven [ɪ'levn]
2	two [tu:]	12	twelve [twelv]
3	three [θri:]	13	thirteen ['θɜ:'ti:n]
4	four [fɔ:]	14	fourteen ['fɔ:'ti:n]
5	five [faɪv]	15	**fifteen** [fɪf'ti:n]
6	six [sɪks]	16	sixteen [sɪks'ti:n]
7	seven ['sevn]	17	seventeen [sevn'ti:n]
8	eight [eɪt]	18	**eighteen** [eɪ'ti:n]
9	nine [naɪn]	19	nineteen [naɪn'ti:n]
10	ten [ten]	20	twenty ['twentɪ]
21	twenty-one ['twentɪ'wʌn]	200	two hundred
22	twenty-two ['twentɪ'tu:]	220	two hundred and twenty
23	twenty-three ['twentɪ'θri:]	1,000	a (one) thousand ['θaʊzənd]
30	thirty ['θɜ:tɪ]		
40	**forty** ['fɔ:tɪ]	1,000,000	a/one million ['mɪljən]
50	**fifty** ['fɪftɪ]	2,320,000	two million three hundred and twenty thousand
60	sixty ['sɪkstɪ]		
70	seventy ['sevntɪ]		
80	**eighty** ['eɪtɪ]		
90	ninety ['naɪntɪ]		
100	a (one) hundred [ə'hʌndrəd]		

§§ 287, 290 ►AB 4

C 7

£6	per a	week

(§ 125)

C 8 **by** car/bus/... but: on foot (§ 126)

C 9 you can see = *(German:) ... man ...* § 154

D1 Right or wrong?

1 Jane's room is very comfortable.
2 Jane's room is near Holland Park.
3 Jane's room is five minutes from the Zoo.
4 Jane can see the animals from her room.
5 There's a lot of traffic in the street in front of Jane's room.
6 The African student's room is in Chester Terrace.
7 His room is very quiet at night.
8 He can see the park.
9 From his room he can see the entrance to the Underground.
10 There is a quiet street in front of his house.

D2 **There is** or **There are**?

1 ... a garage near Jim's house.
2 ... a lot of fine old trees in his garden.
3 ... three bedrooms in his house.
4 ... a very modern kitchen.
5 ... a quiet street in front of his house.
6 ... a park near Jim's house.
7 ... 28 flats in this block in Central London.
8 ... a lot of fine old houses near Regent's Park.

D3 **Is there** or **Are there**?

1 ... two or three bedrooms?
2 ... a toilet?
3 ... a basement in the house?
4 ... two or three windows in the living-room?
5 ... a TV?
6 ... a lot of trees in the garden?
7 ... a garage for my wife's car, too?
8 ... a lot of traffic in front of the house?
9 ... two bathrooms?

D 4 *Find the right answer:*

1 How many bedrooms are there in the house in Blackheath?

2 How much is the house in Blackheath?

3 How many trees can you see from your living-room window?

4 How much is that car over there?

5 How many rooms are there in your flat?

6 How much is a flat in the modern block in Central London?

a It's £135 a week.
b There are flats from £75 to £225 a week.
c There are three.
d There are two bedrooms, a living room, a kitchen and a bathroom.
e You can see three.
f The Mini? It's £800.

D 5 The new flat

Unit 3 **Shopping – where and when?**

A1 Meet Mr and Mrs Singh

You are at Frankfurt airport and you hear this:

– Meet Mr and Mrs Singh. They are from India.
  – How do you do?
    – How do you do?
– And these are their children, Nina, Anu and Ashok.
  – Hello.

Can you tell a friend who these families are and where they are from?

A 2

Win a weekend trip to London and a BCM 1200 your ideal family car!

Can you answer these questions?

You can win a weekend in London and your **BCM 1200** from British Car Makers:

YES	NO	
☐	☐	The Watersons live in an old house in King Street.
☐	☐	In front of their house there is a park.
☐	☐	They can see a lot of trees from their living-room window.
☐	☐	They like British cars.
☐	☐	Their car is a **BCM 1200**.

(Family name) (First name) (Address)

To: British Car Makers/'Weekend trip to London'/Coventry CV3 1DG

And what about you and your family/friend?

– We live in. . . .
In front of our house . . . .
From . . . living-room window . . . can see . . . .
. . . like . . . .
. . . car is . . . .

▸ AB 3

A 3 What's the time, please?

5.00 a.m.
It's 5 o'clock
in the morning.

3.00 p.m.
It's 3 o'clock
in the afternoon.

6.00 p.m.
It's 6 o'clock
in the evening.

10.00 p.m.
It's 10 o'clock.

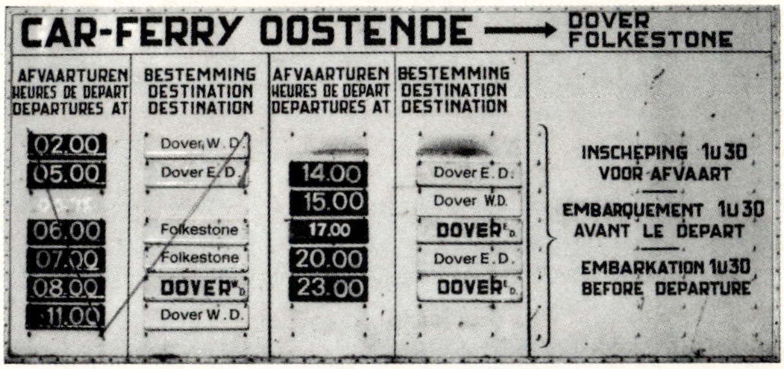

– When's the next boat to . . . ?

– It's at eleven o'clock.

– Is there a boat	in the afternoon?
	in the evening?
	in the morning?

– Yes, there's one at . . . .
No, there isn't.

A 4 What time is it, please?

– It's . . .

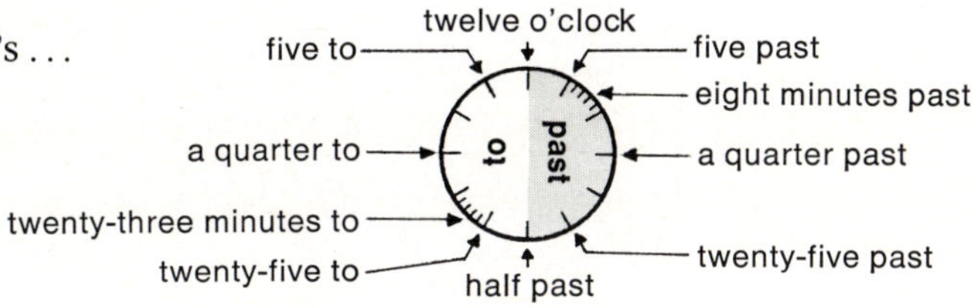

– When must you leave your house/flat for your English class?

– What time is your	bus	after your English class?
	. . .	

► AB 4, C 4, C 5

Lond
Hull

London King's Cross→
Hull

	King's Cross dep.	Hull arr.
	01.15	07.32
	05.50	10.10
125	08.00	10.56
	08.04	**11.28**
	09.04	12.40
	09.30	12.40
125	11.35	14.33
	12.04	**15.32**
	12.45	16.40
	13.25	16.40
	14.45	18.33
	15.45	19.30
	16.04	19.30
	16.42	**20.06**
	18.00	21.00
125	19.00	21.42
	19.50	00.06
	22.30	04.14
	23.55	04.53
	23.55	05.16

125 Inter-City 125 trains

A 5 When's the next train to Hull?

– When's the next train to Hull?

– At nine oh four.

– Is there a train in the afternoon?

– Yes, there's one at a quarter to four.

▸ AB 9

A 6 Listen, please

What time is the next train to Hull? (a) 4.30 (b) 9.30 (c) 5.30

A 7 Listen, please

destination	time	flight	gate
VIENNA	18:35	OS 456	14
OSLO	18:50	SK 512	12
FRANKFURT	19:00	LH 037	
BRUSSELS	19:20	SN 612	11

Where must you go for flight LH 037 to Frankfurt?

A 8 **Excuse me, where can I get jeans, please?**

– Excuse me,

where can I	get	jeans	, please?
	find	T-shirts	
		shoes	
		a blouse	
		a skirt	
		radios	
		records	
		a suitcase	
		picture postcards	
		. . .	

– On the . . . floor.

– Thank you very much.

1 A 9 Where can I get stamps?

– Excuse me, is there a	post office shoe shop bank record shop book shop chemist's radio shop flower shop	near here?

– Yes,	go along this street and it's the	fifth fourth third second	on the right.
	it's here, next to this shop.		
	go along this street and it's the	second third	on the left.

– Thank you very much.

– Not at all.

– Excuse me, where can I	get buy	jeans T-shirts a blouse stamps picture postcards . . .	near here?

– At	Jean Machine. the post office. the record shop.	Go . . . and it's the	sixth . . .	. . . .

► D 6, AB 6, AB 7, AB 10

A 10 Listen, please

You are at the information desk of a department store.

Where can you get these?

1	Men's shoes	on the . . . floor.
2	Children's clothes	on the . . . floor.
3	Books	on the . . . floor.

A 11 Listen, please

What is the question?

– Excuse me, where is . . . ?

A 12

► D 5

A 13 That's nice!

– This That	suitcase skirt ...	is nice. How much is it?
These Those	jeans flowers ...	are nice. How much are they?

– It's .... .
They're .... .

– Oh, that's very expensive.		
Good. I'd like	this one, these,	please.

► D 7, AB 8

2 **B**

Meier's London – a cheap weekend trip?

Mr and Mrs Meier are on a weekend shopping trip to London. They are with Harvey Miller, an English friend from London.

Mr M. – Where can I get stamps for these picture postcards, Harvey?

H.M. – There's a post office over there on the right.

Mrs M. – Are the shops open this afternoon?

H.M. – Well, a lot of shops are open from nine thirty to half past five on Saturday.

Mrs M. – Good. I'd like to buy a record for Peter and shoes for Alfred and me.

H.M. – Alright. We can get the record from HMV, then we can go to Selfridges for the shoes.

Mrs M. – Oh, and I must get a blouse and a skirt for Ingrid, and a T-shirt for Peter.

H.M. – You can get those at Marks and Spencers.

Mr M. – Alright. First we go to the post office, then we can buy the clothes, and after that we can go to HMV for the record. And when can we go sightseeing?

H.M. – Well, what about Sunday morning when the shops are closed?

Mrs M. – But on Sunday morning I must go to Petticoat Lane.

Sunday evening, at Heathrow Airport.

Mr M. – Are the records for Peter in this parcel, Harvey?

H.M. – Pardon?

Mr M. – The records for Peter, are they in this parcel?

H.M. – No, they aren't, but what about those parcels?

Mrs M. – No, they aren't here. There are only the books, and the blouse.

Mr M. – And what about that bag over there?

Mrs M. – That's a bag from the jeans shop in King's Road. They can't be in there. Are they in one of our suitcases?

Mr M. – No, they aren't.

Mrs M. – Oh, Harvey, they must be in the Underground. What can we do now?

Mr M. – We must go to the lost property office.

Mrs M. – But it's closed on Sunday.

H.M. – That's alright. I can go there on Monday for you.

Mr M. – Seven expensive records. You and your cheap weekend in London!

► D 1, AB 1

C1 We – you – they

1 Where are **you and your girlfriend** from, Peter?
– **We** are from Germany.
2 Excuse me, Mr and Mrs Meier, where are **you** from?
3 Where are **the Meiers**? – **They** are in London.

we write	*we say*
we are	we're
you are	you're
they are	they're
are not	aren't

§§ (28), 153

C2 Our – your – their

1 **Mrs Meier**: – **Alfred**, where are **our** suitcases?
2 – **Peter and Barbara**, are these **your** books?
3 **The Meiers** meet **their** friend Harvey Miller.

§ 151 ►D 3, D 4

C3 What time is it?

– It's 7 o'clock in the morning.	– It's 7 a.m.
– It's 3 o'clock in the afternoon.	– It's 3 p.m.
– It's 6 o'clock in the evening.	– It's 6 p.m.
– It's 10 o'clock.	– It's 10 p.m.

§ 291

C4

11.00	eleven o'clock
11.05	five (minutes) past eleven
11.08	eight minutes past eleven
11.10	ten (minutes) past eleven
11.15	a quarter past eleven
11.20	twenty (minutes) past eleven
11.25	twenty-five (minutes) past eleven
11.30	half past eleven
11.35	twenty-five (minutes) to twelve
11.45	a quarter to twelve
11.52	eight minutes to twelve
11.55	five (minutes) to twelve
12.00	twelve o'clock

( ) = You can say 'Five minutes past eleven' or 'Five past eleven'.

§ 291

C5 W-questions – asking the time

What's the time	= What time is it?
What time is your bus?	= When is your bus?

(§ 167) ►AB 9

C 6 CAN – CANNOT ['kænɒt]/CANT [kɑ:nt]

I You He/She We They	can cannot	buy get	jeans stamps	in a department store.

we write	*we say*
cannot	can't

§§ 4, (61, 62) ▶AB 5

C 7 MUST

I You He/She We They	must	leave	the house at six.

§§ 4, (71) ▶AB 6

C 8 W-questions

Where	can	I	get	stamps?
When	must	you	leave	the house?
What	must	they	buy	first?
What	can	you	see	from your window?

§ 9 ▶D 6

C 9 Yes/no-questions and short answers

Can	I	buy	stamps	in a department store?
Can	you	hear	the animals	from the zoo?

– No, you can't.
– Yes, I can.

§ 7 ▶D 2

C 10

1	one	1st	the **first**	[fɜ:st]
2	two	2nd	the **second**	['sekənd]
3	three	3rd	the **third**	[θɜ:d]
4	four	4th	the fourth	[fɔ:θ]
5	five	5th	the **fifth**	[fɪfθ]
6	six	6th	the sixth	[sɪksθ]
7	seven	7th	the seventh	['sevnθ]
8	eight	8th	the **eighth**	[eɪtθ]
9	nine	9th	the **ninth**	[naɪnθ]
10	ten	10th	the tenth	[tenθ]

§§ 292 ▶AB 7

C 11

(**Whose**?) Peter'**s** records — children'**s** clothes (… **for** children)

The Meie**rs'** suitcases — men'**s** shoes

at the chemist's = at the chemist's ~~shop~~

§§ 119, 120

C 12 This : that = these : those

§ 135 ►D 5

C 13 W-questions

How much **is it**? – **It's** £1.30.

How much **are they**? – **They are** £68.

(§ 137) ►D 7

D 1 Right or wrong?

1 The Meiers meet their friend in Germany.
2 The Meiers are in London for two days.
3 Shops are closed on Saturday afternoon in England.
4 You can get T-shirts and blouses at Marks and Spencers.
5 Shops in London are closed on Sunday morning.
6 The jeans for Peter are not in the Meiers' suitcases.
7 They go to the lost property office at Heathrow airport.
8 On Sunday evening the Meiers are in Germany again.

D 2 Can you answer these questions?

Can you	buy a stamp in a department store? go shopping in London on Saturday afternoon? buy a record at HMV on Sunday morning? buy shoes at Selfridges?
Can the Meiers	go to the lost property office on Sunday? go sight-seeing on Sunday?
Can Mr Meier	get a stamp at the post office? find the records in their suitcase?

– Yes,	you they he	can.	– No,	you they he	can't.

D 3 **They** or **their**?

1 The Meiers must buy clothes for ... children.

2 The Meiers are at the airport. ... can't find the records for Peter in ... suitcases.

3 Jim and Fred are students. ... rooms are in the basement. From ... windows ... can see the entrance to the Underground.

4 Ingrid and Barbara are German. ... live in an old house near the zoo. From ... window ... can see the trees in the park. And sometimes ... can hear the animals in the zoo.

D 4 **We** or **our**?

Susan	**Peter**
– Are ... near ... hotel?	– No, ... aren't. ... are in Onslow Square. ... hotel is in Onslow Gardens.
– But Onslow Square is near Onslow Gardens.	– Of course it is. But ... aren't near ... hotel. That's Old Brompton Road over there.
– Of course ...'re near ... hotel. Old Brompton Road is near Onslow Gardens.	– There's an entrance to the Underground over there.
– It's 'South Kensington'. ... hotel is only five minutes from here.	– You're right. ... are at South Kensington. That's Old Brompton Road, and Onslow Gardens is the fifth street on the left. And over there's the shop where ... buy ... cigarettes.

► AB 2, AB 3

D 5 **These** or **those**?

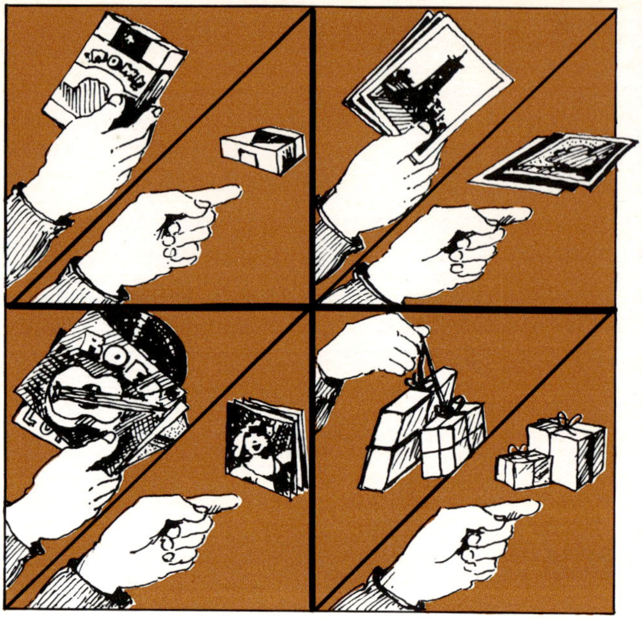

– Are . . . your cigarettes?

– No, they aren't.
. . . are my cigarettes.

D 6 *Look at* A9 *again please.*

– What can you	get buy	in the	first second fourth sixth	shop on the left?
			second third	shop on the right?

– (It's a . . . shop.) You can get . . . there.

D 7 **How much is** or **How much are**?

1 . . . the flat near Holland Park?
2 . . . the pictures over there?
3 . . . this lamp?
4 . . . this lighter?
5 . . . the flowers over there?
6 . . . the suitcase?
7 . . . a room in the basement?
8 . . . the two rooms in the basement?

► AB 8

Unit 4 Family life

A1 Can I borrow it, please?

– Excuse me, have you got a pen?

– No, I'm sorry, I haven't, but I've got a pencil.

– Can I borrow it for a moment, please?

– Yes, of course. Here you are.

A2 Have you got a car?

– Have you got a car, Doris?
– Yes, I have.
No, I haven't.

– How old is it?
– It's . . . years old.

– Is it a Volkswagen?
– Yes, it is.
No, it isn't. It's an Opel.

– Have you got a car, too, Peter?
– Yes, I have.

– Is it an Opel, too?
– Yes, it is.
No, it isn't. It's a . . . .

A3

– Has your	husband wife . . .	got a car, too?		– Yes, No,	he/she	has. hasn't.
– Is your	husband's wife's . . .	car an Opel, too?		– Yes, it is. No, it isn't. It's a		

► AB 2, AB 3

A 4

– Have you got a lot of	records? stamps? . . . ?		– Yes, I have. No, I haven't.

– Has your	husband . . .	got a lot of . . . ?	– Yes, he has. . . . .

1 A 5 Can you help me?

– Can you help	me, us,	please?

– What's the matter?

– There's something wrong with	my our	car. radio. . . . .

– Well, let's see.			
I'm sorry, I can't help you. But	Dick Helen Jim and Pat	can, ask	him. her. them.

► D 2

A 6 Can I help you?

– Can I help you?

– Yes, please.
Thank you, that's very kind of you.
No, thank you, it's alright.

A 7 The Brown family

Edward and
Victoria Brown

Hugh and Helen Brown
and their children

Charlotte and Patrick Howard

Ralph Howard

Daisy Howard

Hugh is Helen's . . . . Helen is Hugh's . . . .

John is their son.
Jill, Janice, and Jennifer are their daughters.
Hugh and Helen have four children.

Ralph Howard is Helen's brother.
Daisy is her sister.

Edward Brown is Hugh's father. He is John's grandfather.
Victoria is Hugh's mother. She is Helen's mother-in-law.
Charlotte and Patrick Howard are Helen's parents.

Ralph is John's uncle.
Daisy is his aunt.

Who's John?	*Jennifer* *Helen* *Edward*	– He's my . . . . – He's my . . . . – He's my . . . .
Who's Hugh?	*Helen* *Edward* *Ralph* *John* *Patrick*	– He's my . . . . – He's my . . . . – He's my . . . . – He's my . . . . – He's our . . . .
Who's Helen?	*Hugh* *Jill and John* *Charlotte* *Daisy*	– She's my . . . . – She's our . . . . – She's our . . . . – She's my . . . .
Who are Patrick and Charlotte?	*Helen* *John and Jill*	– They're my . . . . – They're our . . . .

– How many brothers have you got? – I've got . . . .
– Has your wife/husband got a . . . ? – Yes, ...

A 8 What day is it today?

we write
5th April, 1975 *or:* April 5, 1975; *or:* 5 April 75

– What day is it today?
– It's Monday, 25th November.

– When is your birthday?
– My birthday is on 2nd May.

we say
The fifth of April, nineteen seventy-five. *or:* April the fifth, ...

► AB 5, AB 6

A 9 Presents, presents, presents

Mr White is back from a business trip. The Whites have got four children. They ask him:

– What have you got for us, Dad?

Have you got	a piece of chewing-gum a bar of chocolate . . . a puzzle	for	us? me?

It's Mrs White's birthday.
Mr White has got a lot of things for her:

He has got	. . . . . . a ticket for a concert . . .	for her.

It's Christmas.
This is what Mrs White has got for her husband:

She has got	a new . . . . . . an umbrella . . .	for him.

► D 3

A 10 I've got a present for you

– What	birthday Christmas	presents have you got for your	husband? wife? children? . . . ?

– I've got	a record jeans . . .	for	him. her. them.
Nothing (yet).			

– And what has	he she	got for you?

– I've got no idea.

I think	he's got . . .	. . . for me.

– And what have your parents got for you and your	husband? . . . ?

– I think they've got . . . for us.

► AB 4

A 11 Thank you

– That's What	a nice	pen. lighter. . . . .

– It's for you.

– For me?

– Yes, for you.

– Oh, thank you.

3 A 12

– Is there	a good a new	film	on TV on at the cinema	tonight? tomorrow night? this week?	
				on	Monday? Tuesday? . . . ?

– Yes, there is.
No, there isn't.
There's | an old American film on | tonight.
. . . | . . . .

– Is it | an old / a good | film or | a new / a bad | film?

– I think it's a | new / bad / . . . | film.

A 13 Listen, please

a

b

c

1 = picture . . .

2 = picture . . .

3 = picture . . .

B Good night, Jenny

– Dad, what have you got there?
– It's a puzzle for you, dear.
– Can we do it now?
– Oh dear! This is a very difficult puzzle. It has got a thousand pieces. We can do it when I've got more time.
– Has Mummy got time to do it with me?
– No, dear, she hasn't. Mummy and I are going to the cinema tonight. We must leave in ten minutes. – Helen, where's my lighter? I can't find it. Have you got it? Alright, Jenny, we can do the puzzle tomorrow night.

– Jim, have you got the tickets?
– Yes, of course I have, dear. Have you got the umbrella? It's raining.
– No, not yet.
– Dad, why can't we play Memory?
– I haven't got time now. We can play Memory tomorrow night.
– Jim, the baby-sitter is coming. Have you got enough money for her and for the bus?
– But we're going by car.
– Oh yes, of course. Have you got the keys?
– Dad, have you got a bar of chocolate for me?
– No, I haven't!
– Has Mummy got chewing-gum, then?
– Helen, have you got chewing-gum for Jenny?
– But Jenny, you know that chocolate and chewing-gum aren't good for your teeth.
– Oh, Mummy, chewing-gum isn't bad for the teeth.

– Jim, you can take that letter with you. There's a post office near the cinema. Here's Karen. How are you, Karen?
– Good evening, Mrs Gray. Hello, Jenny.
– Oh, hello, Karen. How are you? – The letter? – I've got it. Here it is. Can we go now?
– Alright. Night-night, Jenny. Bye-bye, Karen. There's chewing-gum in the kitchen for Jenny and a drink for you.
– Fine, thank you, Mrs Gray.
– Night-night, Mummy. Night, Dad.
– Night, Jenny. We can do the puzzle tomorrow night.
– But Jim, we've got tickets for the Bach concert tomorrow night.
– Oh, Daddy!
– I've got a lot of time at the weekend, Jenny.
– Come on, Jim. It's late.

► D 1, AB 1, AB 7

C 1 HAVE GOT – HAS GOT
HAVEN'T GOT – HASN'T GOT

I	**have**	**got**	a pen, but I **haven't got** a pencil.
You	**have**	**got**	a nice hand-bag. Is it from France?
He	**has**	**got**	a picture postcard, but he **hasn't got** a stamp for it.
She	**has**	**got**	a new blouse but she **hasn't got** a new coat.
It	**has**	**got**	a thousand pieces.
We	**have**	**got**	a lot of time, it's only six.
You	**have**	**got**	a very nice house.
They	**have**	**got**	a house in Ireland.

we write	*we say*
I have got he has got ...	I've got he's got ...

§ 33 ►D 4, D 5

C 2 Yes/no-questions and short answers

Have you got a lot of records? – Yes, I have.
No, I haven't.

Has your husband got a car? – Yes, he has.
No, he hasn't.

§§ 7, 18 ►D 4

C 3 W-questions

What have you got for me?

What has your husband got for you?

but: What presents have you got for your wife? *(Was für . . . ?)*

What day is it today?

§§ 9, (162)

C 4

Can you see	me?
I can't help	you.
There's Peter. Ask	him.
There's Jane. Ask	her.
Can you see	it?
Can you help	us?
Sorry, I can't help	you.
Jim, can you help	them?

Have you got a bar of chocolate	for me?
No, I'm afraid I haven't got time	for you.
Is his wife	with him?
Is her husband	with her?
Have you got two tickets	for us?
Tom and Mary, here's a puzzle	for you.
Where are the Millers? I've got a parcel	for them.

§ 153 ►D 2, D 3

C 5

Monday	['mʌndɪ]
Tuesday	['tju:zdɪ]
Wednesday	['wenzdɪ]
Thursday	['θɜ:zdɪ]
Friday	['fraɪdɪ]
Saturday	['sætədɪ]
Sunday	['sʌndɪ]

► D 6

C 6

The months of the year

January	['dʒænjʊərɪ]	July	[dʒʊ'laɪ]
February	['febrʊərɪ]	August	['ɔ:gəst]
March	[mɑ:tʃ]	September	[sep'tembə]
April	['eɪprəl]	October	[ɒk'təʊbə]
May	[meɪ]	November	[nəʊ'vembə]
June	[dʒu:n]	December	[dɪ'sembə]

§ 293 ► AB 6

C 7

11th	eleventh	20th	twentieth ['twentɪəθ]
12th	twelfth [twelfθ]	21st	twenty-first
13th	thirteenth	30th	thirtieth

§ 292

C 8

Jennifer is Hugh and Helen's child
The Browns have got four children.

I think I have a bad tooth.
Chocolate isn't good for your teeth.

wife	wives
housewife	housewives
man	men
businessman	businessmen

(§ 109)

D 1 *Read* 4/B *again. Who says what?*

D 2 *Fill in* me, you, him, her, *etc.*

1 – This puzzle is very difficult, Dad, can you help . . . , please?

2 – Molly is only 16, we can't let . . . have the car.

3 – Can I help . . . , madam?

4 – Fred can't find his lighter. I'm afraid I can't help . . . .

5 – Betty can't find her keys. I'm afraid I can't help . . . .

6 – We can't find the entrance to the Underground. Can you help . . . ?
– No, I'm afraid I can't help . . . .

7 – You meet Alex Dupont at the bar. Ask . . . where Colette is.

D 3 *Fill in* me, you, him, her, *etc.*

1 – This is for your wife. – Thank you, but my wife isn't with . . . .

2 – Is your husband with . . . , Mrs Finch? – No, he's at home.

3 – Is her husband with . . . in Paris? – No, she's there with her sister.

4 – These flowers are for Jane, and this record is for . . . , too.

5 – Where's Peter? I've got a book for . . . .

6 – Are your friends with . . . , Peter and Mary? – No, they aren't with . . . .

7 – The Rolling Stones are in London, but Mick Jagger isn't with . . . .

► AB 4

D 4 **Have** or **has?**

1 – Bill . . . got a nice flat.

2 – . . . you got the umbrella, Jack?

3 – Fred and I . . . got tickets for the concert.

4 – Your wife . . . got a letter for you.

5 – The lady at the reception . . . got a letter for you.

6 – We . . . got a new car.

7 – . . . you and Bob got a baby-sitter for Tuesday night?

8 – . . . they got picture postcards at the bookshop over there?

► AB 2

D 5 **Haven't** or **hasn't?**

1 – I . . . got enough money.
2 – Jim . . . got his wife with him.
3 – Bill and Helen . . . got enough time for Jenny.
4 – Sheila . . . got a baby-sitter for tonight.
5 – Jane . . . got a new boyfriend.
6 – We . . . got a colour TV.

► AB 3

D 6

LONDON — PERTH

		Mon	Tue	Wed	Thu	Fri	Sat	Sun
Kensington Olympia	dep	1055	0955	1055	1030	1055	0955	—
Perth	arr	1825	1725	1825	1800	1825	1725	—
Perth	dep	0955	1055	0955	0955	1055	1055	—
Kensington Olympia	arr	1805	1905	1805	1805	1905	1905	—

– Is there a train from . . . to . . . on . . . ?
– Yes, there's one at . . . .
No, ...

► AB 5

D 7

– Have you got [a: the tickets?]

– Yes, of course I have. And have you got [b: the umbrella?]

– No, I haven't got [c: it] yet.

	a	b	c
1	the cigarettes	your hand-bag	it *or* them
2	the letters	the stamps	
3	the keys to the car	your coat	
4	enough money	the tickets for the cinema	

Unit 5 Jobs and free time

1 A1

Can I speak to Mr Brown?

– Hello.

– Is that 335 3022?

– No, this is 335 3032.

– Sorry, wrong number.

– 335 3022.

– Hello, is that John?

– Yes, speaking.

– Hello, John. This is Helen.

– Hello, Helen.

– Littleton & Sons.

– Good morning. Can I speak to Mr Brown, please?

– I'm sorry, he's speaking on the other phone.

– It's alright. I can ring him this afternoon.

– Thank you. Goodbye.

– Goodbye.

A 2 Listen, please

1 What's her number? Susan Webb a) 0272/43709 b) 02722/4379	**2** What's their number? Crawley & Sons . . . .
3 Peter is a) at home b) not at home	**4** Mr Brown is a) in. b) out.

A 3 Can you say it again, please?

– My name is Sharma.

– Pardon?

– Sharma. My name's Sharma.

– Ah, yes, Mr Farmer.

– No, not Farmer – Sharma.

– I'm sorry, it's a bad line. Can you spell it, please?

– S for Samuel, H, A, R, M for Mary, A.

– Oh, I'm sorry, Mr Sharma.

B	Benjamin	N	Nancy
D	Dublin	P	Peter
F	Frederick	S	Samuel
M	Mary	T	Tom

A 4

– Hello.

– Hello, Carl. This is Andrew. I'm phoning from the reception desk. What are you doing at the moment?

– Oh, nothing. I'm just drinking a cup of tea.

– I'm just leaving for the boat show. Are you coming along?

– Yes, of course.

– Is that Alex Dupont? Look, he's taking a taxi. Hello, Alex! Are you going to the boat show, too?

– Yes, I am.

– And what about your wife?

– Oh, she's going to the zoo.

– What's	Carl Wagner	doing?	Is he going to the boat show?
	Andrew Harris		
	Mr Dupont		Is he going by Underground?
	Mrs Dupont		Is she going to the boat show?

A 5

– Hello.

– Hello, this is Peggy May speaking.

– Hello, Peggy. How are you?

– Fine, thanks. And you and Karen? What are you two doing at the moment?

– Why? We're sitting at home. We're watching TV. And you and Mike?

– Oh, we're just going out. We're going to the cinema to see a Western.

– We're just watching a Western on TV. Clint Eastwood is in it. The cowboys are just leaving the bar. They're – – –

– Clint Eastwood? He's great! I'd like to see that.

– Come over, then – but hurry.

– Alright. See you in a minute. 'Bye.

– What's	Karen's husband Peggy	doing?
What are	Peggy and Mike Karen and her husband the cowboys	

– He's . . . . She's	
Peggy and Mike Karen and her husband They	are . . . .

► AB 3

A 6 Looking at pictures of Mr and Mrs Ferguson's first holiday in Italy

Mr and Mrs Ferguson are back from their first holiday in Italy. Mrs Ferguson and one of her neighbours are looking at pictures of the Fergusons' holiday. Mrs Ferguson is talking about the pictures:

1

– This is our hotel room in Rimini. Here we're looking out of the window. It's a very modern hotel, isn't it?

2

– Here we're lying in the sun. Can you see us? No? Over there, near the ice-cream stand.

3

– And here Fred is eating spaghetti. It's very difficult for an Englishman, you know.

4

– Here Fred ... picture postcards.

5

– Here Fred is opening a bottle of wine! Yes, wine! Fred and red wine!

6

– Fred ... boccia.

7

– Here we ... in the garden of our hotel. Fred ... *white* wine here.

8

– And here we're in Venice. I'm going into St. Mark's.

9

– Here Fred ... a bar with a bottle of you-know-what.

10

– And here I'm standing near the famous tower of Pisa. It was very difficult for Fred to take this picture.

11

– Here Fred is speaking Italian. What a holiday!

Now you are	*Fred.* *a friend of the Fergusons.*	*Talk about the pictures, please.*

A 7

– What's your	husband wife . . .	doing at the moment?

– I think he's/she's	eating dinner. drinking a glass of whisky. watching TV. listening to the radio. working. playing. . . . sitting . . . .

A 8

I'm a secretary

It's eight o'clock. Brenda is hurrying to the bus.

It's a quarter past eight. The bus is late. Brenda is getting on the No. 78 bus.

Now it's half past eight. Brenda is sitting at her desk.

And now it's a quarter to nine. Brenda is working.

It's ten to nine. She . . . Miller & Sons.

It's twenty past nine. Brenda . . . .

. . . . Brenda . . . again.

. . . . Brenda . . . the office.

It's . . . . She . . . a shop.

It's . . . . She . . . home by bus.

It's . . . . She . . . dinner.

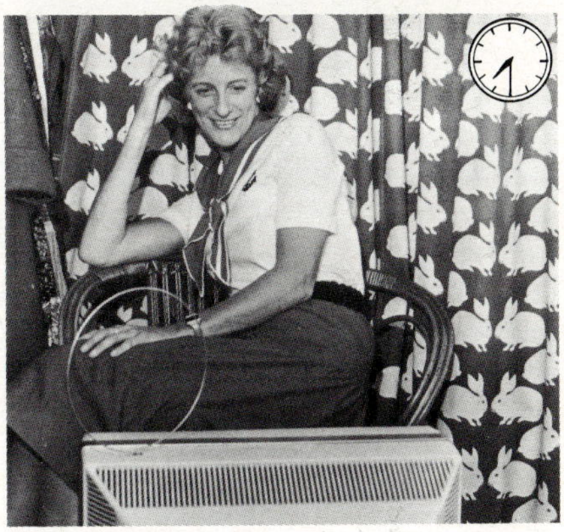

It's . . . . She . . . .

► AB 2

A 9 Jobs

1 It's a Western, it's a ■ ■ ■ [■] ■ ■ film.

2 Colette Dupont is a ■ ■ [■] ■ ■ ■ ■ ■ ■ .

3 Brenda is a ■ ■ ■ [■] ■ ■ ■ ■ ■ .

4 Andrew Harris is ICC's sales ■ ■ ■ ■ [■] ■ ■ .

5 P O [L] I C E M A N .

6 Carl Wagner is a German business ■ [■] ■ .

7 Patrick Mulligan is an ■ ■ ■ ■ [■] .

8 He's climbing through a window. He's a

– What's your job? – I'm a . . . .

3 **B**

The Burglar

– Hello, officer? There's a man in our neighbour's garden. He's standing near a window of the house. He's – – – Yes? – – – Yes, I'm in my living-room. I'm looking out of the window. – – – My name? My name is Glenda Grey. The man is opening the window! He's – – – My address? Oh, yes, of course. My address is 15, West Close.

Oh dear, the man is climbing through the window. – – – My job? Officer, what has my job to do with this?! The man is turning on the lights in the bedroom. – – – My husband's name?! My husband's name is Roger. – – – No, he isn't at home. He's at the office. He's working. – – – My husband's job? Officer, the man is leaving the bedroom and going into the living-room. What has my husband's job – – – Yes, of course, you're writing all this down. Fine. But the man in our neighbour's garden is taking something from a desk. Listen, this is serious!

Now he's opening the door to the kitchen. – – – No, it's **not** our neighbour! – – – Yes, I can see him. Officer, the man is leaving the house again! – – – My neighbour's name and address?! 12, West Close. – – – Yes, that's right, it's Lord Ormsby's summer house. – – – Yes, officer. Alright. But please hurry.

► D 1, AB 1

C 1 THE PROGRESSIVE FORM

I	**am**	watch**ing**	television **at the moment.**
You	**are**	sitt**ing**	on a very old chair **at the moment.**
He	**is**	speak**ing**	to his girlfriend.
She	**is**	go**ing**	to the zoo.
It	**is**	rain**ing**	.
We	**are**	watch**ing**	an old Western **at the moment.**
You	**are**	drink**ing**	my whisky.
They	**are**	leav**ing**	the cinema.

§§ 29, 50, 89 ►D 2, D 3

we write	
sit – sitting get – getting . . . – . . .	leave – leaving come – coming write – writing take – taking . . . – . . .
and: lie – lying	

we write	*we say*
I am watching	I'm watching
He is speaking	He's speaking
It is raining	It's raining

C 2 Yes/no-questions and short answers

– **Are you** go**ing** home by bus? – Yes, **I am.**
No, **I'm not.**

– **Is it** rain**ing**? – Yes, **it is.**
No, **it isn't.**

§§ 7, 18

C 3 W-questions

What **are you** do**ing** at the moment?
Where **is Alex** go**ing**?

► AB 3, AB 4

C 4

I'm not speak**ing** German at the moment. (= I am not . . .)
We aren't watch**ing** TV at the moment. (= We are not . . .)
He isn't speak**ing** to you at the moment. (= He is not . . .)

§ 28

C 5

1 What's the number of your house?
It must be in one of our suitcases.

2 a piece of chewing-gum
a bar of chocolate
a cup of tea
a bottle of wine

§ 121 ►AB 5

D1 *Find out and write down the police officer's questions in* B.

D2 **A picture story**

1

This is Mr King. What's he doing? He . . . .

2

What is the man at the house doing? He

3

Now he . . . .

4

5

6

7

8

9

10

– What are you doing here?!

– I'm . . . whisky, officer.

– And who are you?!

– My name's Jackson, officer. This is my house.

– ? ? ?

– Ah! The window! Well, my wife is at the cinema, and my keys are in her hand-bag.

► AB 2

D 3 Can I speak to John, please?

– Hello.

– Is that 486 22 29?

– Yes.

– Is that [John] speaking? **1**

– No, this is [his brother] . **2**

– Oh, can I speak to [John] then, please? **3**

– No, I'm sorry, [he is shopping with Kate] . **4**

– Can I ring [him] tonight? **5**

– Yes, of course. What's your name, please?

– . . .

– Thank you, goodbye, ...

1
Martha Bill Jane Peter Karen

2
her sister his uncle her mother Alf her daughter

3
Martha Bill or Ann Jane or Cindy your brother your mother

4
playing with the children in the park playing tennis having lunch at a restaurant helping our neighbour having a bath

5
her, him *or* them

Unit 6 Every day...

'Yes . . . yes, I'm alone – well, more or less.'

A1 What people do in the evening

They	often sometimes	read the newspaper. go to the theatre. play with their children. wash their car. . . . .

A2 What do you do in the evening?

<table>
<tr><td rowspan="2">– And</td><td colspan="2">you,</td><td rowspan="2">what do you do in the evening?</td></tr>
<tr><td>you and your</td><td>husband,
friends,
. . . ,</td></tr>
</table>

– I We	always usually often sometimes never	read a book in the evening. . . . .

A3 What does your wife do when you are at night school?

– And what does your	husband . . .	do when you're at night school?

– He She	usually	reads a book watches TV talks to . . . . . . s . . .	when . . . .

► AB 6

A 4 What Martha does every day

1

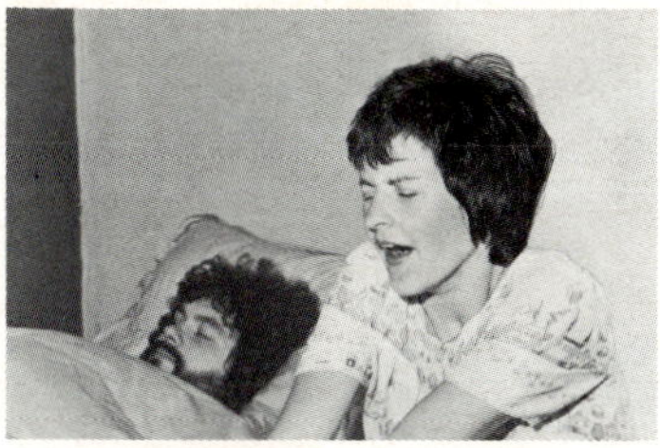

She gets up at 7.

2

She makes breakfast for the family.

3

She makes the beds.

4

She works in the garden.

5

She goes shopping.

6

She does the washing-up.

7

She plays with the children.

8

In the evening she watches TV with her husband.

She does the same things every day.

She	always	gets up at 7.
	usually	. . . .
	. . .	

– Are you a housewife, too? What do you do every day?
– What does your wife do every day?

► AB 2

A 5

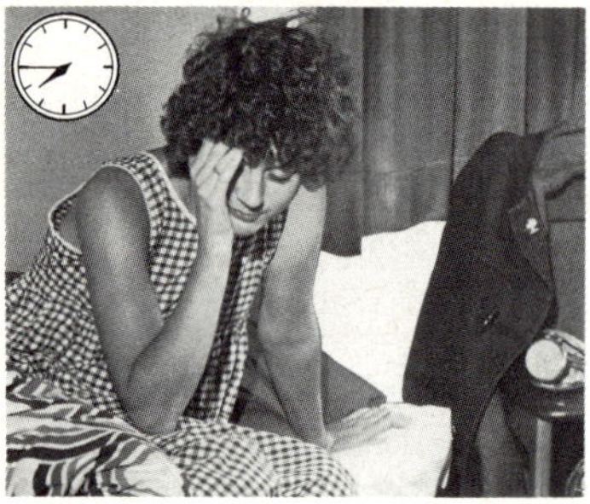

◄
Linda is late today. She is getting up at . . . .
She usually gets up at . . . . ►

►
Linda is eating her breakfast in a hurry.
She usually . . . at . . . . ►►

◄
She . . . at . . . and that's late for her.
She usually . . . . ►

►
Linda . . . the 8.20 bus today.
She usually . . . . ►►

◄
She's starting work at . . . today. She's half an hour late.
She usually . . . at . . . . ►

At the office she usually types a lot of letters. But at the moment she's not typing; she's . . . Miller & Sons.

At 9.30 she usually . . . , but today there's no time for a tea-break. Linda . . . letters.

Linda smokes a lot of cigarettes every morning.
She . . . one at the moment.

► AB 3

◄
It's . . . , and Linda . . . the office.
She usually . . . at . . . . ►

1 A 6 Every day . . .

Write a letter to an English friend about what you do every day.

6, Walton Street,
Oxford OX2 6DP,
2nd June, 1980

Dear Caroline,
Thank you for your letter. This is what my day is like. I get up at . . .

I	get up very early. eat breakfast in a hurry. say 'goodbye' to . . . .

I	start work at . . . o'clock. work in a factory. / a . . . . type a lot of letters. answer phone calls. sell . . . . make . . . . have a coffee-break at . . . . eat lunch in the canteen. leave the . . . at . . . . get home at . . . .

I	make the beds. work in the garden. go shopping. go for a walk with the dog. have a cup of tea with . . . .

I	help my . . . with the housework. . . . . go to bed at . . . .

in the morning
•
first
•
after that
•
then
•
at the office
•
usually
•
sometimes
•
. . .
•
in the evening

Well, that's all for now. I hope to hear from you soon.
With best wishes,
Yours,

► AB 5, D 6

A 7

– What's your	husband . . .	doing at the moment?

– I think	he's she's	watching television. talking to a neighbour. drinking a glass of wine. . . . .

– And why do you think so?

– Because	he she	always often	watches TV talks to our neighbour . . .	in the evening. when I'm here.		
				on	Monday . . .	evening.

► D 3, D 4

A 8 Listen, please

Right or wrong?

1 Jim Broughton often drives the four o'clock train from Watford to Liverpool Street Station.

2 When he gets home he often works in the garden.

3 He always watches television late in the evening.

4 Doris Broughton always gets up with her husband in the morning.

5 When Jim comes home at 2.30 p.m. Doris makes dinner for him.

6 Cindy travels to work by car.

7 At eleven o'clock a colleague makes coffee for Cindy.

8 Cindy has lunch with her boyfriend in the canteen.

9 At lunch she usually talks about clothes and boyfriends.

10 Cindy does her shopping after six o'clock.

A 9 Listen, please

Now listen again, please. What are the missing words?

Jim Broughton is a . . . driver on the London Underground. He often . . . up at . . . o'clock in the . . . and drives an . . . train from Watford to Liverpool Street Station. When he . . . home at . . . , he often . . . in the garden. He . . . to watch television in the . . . but he cannot watch it very late, because he must . . . up so early the next . . . .

Doris Broughton . . . up at . . . every day and . . . breakfast for their daughter Cindy. Then she . . . the beds and does the housework. When her husband comes . . . she . . . a cup of tea for him. In the afternoon she . . . the shopping. At . . . they have dinner. During dinner they always . . . about Jim's day at work. In the evening they sometimes . . . television, but Jim always . . . to bed at . . . .

Cindy is a . . . . Shc usually . . . up at . . . . She . . . breakfast at 7.45. She . . . house at 8.15 and . . . to work by Underground. She usually gets to the office just before . . . . At eleven o'clock she . . . coffee for all her colleagues and then she answers a lot of letters before . . . . She always . . . lunch in the canteen where she . . . to her friends about clothes and boyfriends. She . . . her shopping in the evening after work und usually . . . home at six o'clock.

A 10 Listen, please

You are travelling to Northampton on the M1.

Can you go this way . . . **a**

or this way? **b**

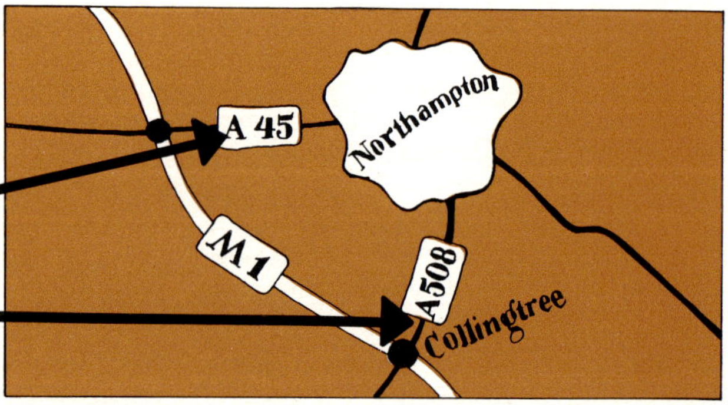

The Strike

B – – Here is the seven o'clock news for today, Friday, 22nd March. Today, on the second day of the strike by London bus and train drivers, there are already traffic-jams on all roads into London. – –

– You and your strike.

– It's not my strike. Who's that in the kitchen?

– It's Cindy. She's making breakfast.

– At seven o'clock?

– Yes, we usually have breakfast at a quarter to eight, but since your strike . . .

– Alright, alright. **I** usually get up at **four** o'clock in the morning.

– Hello, Jim. Working in the garden so early in the morning?

– Ah, it's the strike.

– Why aren't you picketing? You usually picket during strikes.

– Ah, well, you know – – – . It's a nice morning, Stan. How's the family?

– Susan, where's Cindy? She usually starts work at nine.

– Perhaps she's sitting in a traffic-jam or looking for somewhere to park the car.

– But she usually travels to work by Under. . . Oh yes, the strike.

– Yes, everyone is driving to work today.

– What's Brenda doing?

– She's making coffee. Oh, I can see Cindy. She's just coming in.

– Hello, everyone. What a morning! It usually takes me 45 minutes to get here, but today – an hour and a half!

– It's for you, Cindy. It's your father.

– Hello, Dad. What's the matter?

– Oh, nothing really. It's – well, I need the car. There's a strike meeting at six.

– And you can't go by Underground, is that it?

– Look, it's not **my** strike.

– I know, I know.

– You know what I think about it.

– Why aren't you working then?

– I can't be a strike-breaker, can I? But I think that higher wages always mean higher prices. And who pays for all that? Not the bosses in their Rolls-Royces – the man in the street, Cindy – **we** pay for it.

– Alright, Dad, alright. But I must do the shopping for Mum after work. You usually help her on Friday, if you've got the car.

– She's doing the shopping at the moment.

– But she never does the weekend shopping without the car.

– Look, the shops are closed in the afternoon during the strike.

– Oh, I'm sorry, Dad, I'm working. We can talk about all these things this evening.

– Your Mum and I aren't speaking.

– Because of the strike?

– She can't understand my problems. For her the strike only means less money. And you're just like your mother. Alright then, I can walk to the meeting.

▶ D 1, D 2, AB 1, AB 8

C 1 THE SIMPLE PRESENT

I	get	up early every morning.
You	pay	only £2 for that thing at Selfridges.
He	plays	tennis very well.
She	comes	to England every year.
It	rains	a lot in England.
We	watch	TV every evening.
You	find	a lot of very good shops in London.
They	sell	blouses there, too.

§§ 2, 51 ▶ D 3

C 2

play s drive s stand s come s	[z]	get s lik es typ es ...	[s]
watch es wash es	[ɪz]		

§ 52 ►AB 7

C 3

we write and say		
	go [gəʊ]	– goes [gəʊz]
but:	do [duː]	– does [dʌz]
	pay [peɪ]	– pays [peɪz]
but:	say [seɪ]	– says [sez]

we write		
hurr**y**	but:	hurr**ies**

§§ 52, 53

C 4

Every day	Now
I usually speak German.	I'm speaking English at the moment, because my English teacher can't speak German.
I usually go to bed at 10.	It's 10.30 and I'm watching a good film on TV.
I often drink coffee for breakfast.	I've got no coffee this morning; I'm drinking tea.

§§ 88–90, (91) ►D 4

AT THE MOMENT/NOW	⟶	P... Form
OFTEN/EVERY DAY	⟶	S... Present

C 5

		THESE WORDS		
Helen	must	often	get up	early.
John		usually	washes	his car on Saturday.
I	can	sometimes	hear	the animals from the zoo.
Jim		always	comes	home late.
Henry		never	smokes	cigarettes at home.
		USUALLY STAND IN FRONT OF THE	VERB.	

(§§ 90, 201) ►D 5

C 6 Place and time

TIME/(PLACE)		1st: PLACE	2nd: TIME
	Fred goes Tom is	to Italy in London	every year. today.
At 5 o'clock In the afternoon	the Meiers are Jim works	at the airport. in the garden.	
In England	most shops are closed		on Sunday.

§§ 202, 203 ►D 6

C 7 W-questions with do/does

What	**do**	you	**do**	in the evening?
What	**do**	you and your husband	**do**	in the evening?
Why	**do**	you	**think**	so?
What	**does**	your husband	**do**	when you are at night school?
What	**does**	your wife	**do**	every day?

More on w-questions in UNIT 8.

§§ 10, (38, 39)

C 8 Why?

Because **he is** on strike.
Because of **the strike**.

§§ 170, (245), 255

D1 *Read the story about the strike again. Find out who says what, Mrs or Mr Broughton, Cindy, Cindy's boss, Susan, or Stan?*

D2 **The Broughtons on Sunday**

Progressive form or simple present?

1

Jim Broughton ... an Underground train to Uxbridge this morning.

He usually ... the train to Liverpool Street Station.

2

Mrs Broughton ... lunch for the family.

During the week she only ... dinner for them, because they are never at home at lunchtime.

3

Jim Broughton always ... in the garden in the afternoon.

He ... there at the moment.

4

Mrs Broughton often ... to her neighbour.

They ... about Bob's new school.

5

Cindy ... tennis only at the weekend.

Here she ... with Tom Brown, a colleague.

D 3

The Dodsons are a big family. They have all got hobbies.

(wash)	Mr Dodson . . . his car.
(listen)	Mrs Dodson . . . to records.
(read)	Jerry and Betty Dodson . . . a lot of books.
(write)	Jerry . . . stories for a newspaper.
(speak/travel)	Betty . . . French, German and Italian, and . . . a lot.
(play)	Peter and Alf Dodson . . . tennis.
(play)	And Mary Dodson . . . the piano.

▸ AB 2

3

D 4 **The Dodsons on Saturday afternoon**

1

Alf and Peter are playing tennis.

They always . . . on Saturday afternoon.

2

Jerry Dodson . . . .

He . . . .

3

Mary . . . .

She . . . .

4

Betty Dodson . . . a book in Italian.

She . . . .

5

Mrs Dodson isn't listening to records. She . . . for the family.

She never . . . on Saturday afternoon, because she always . . . and . . . the washing-up. What a family!

▸ AB 3

D 5

1 John/in the canteen/eat/never
2 cigarettes/Bill/never/smoke
3 drink/Tom/never/whisky
4 Mary/with the housework/her mother/help/usually
5 leave/the office/Mary/before 5.30/always
6 Mr Smith/often/with his children/play
7 Bob/in the garden/usually/work
8 sometimes/to the theatre/go/we
9 I/travel/to England/often
10 work/in the evening/Jane's husband/often

1 John never eats in the canteen.
2 Bill . . . .
3 . . . .

▸ AB 6

D 6 What they often do

Where	*When*
in front of their TV	after work
in London	at 8 o'clock
in the office	every year
in the park	in the evening
to Italy	on Sunday afternoon

	When		*Where*	*When*
1	. . .	a lot of people eat	. . .	. . . .
2	. . .	Cathy starts work	. . .	. . . .
3	. . .	a lot of people go for a walk	. . .	. . . .
4	. . .	the Meiers go	. . .	. . . .
5	. . .	German tourists buy a lot of souvenirs	. . .	. . . .

D 7 Can I speak to Mike, please?

Unit 7 The quality of life

A1 Be careful!

A2 Don't . . . !

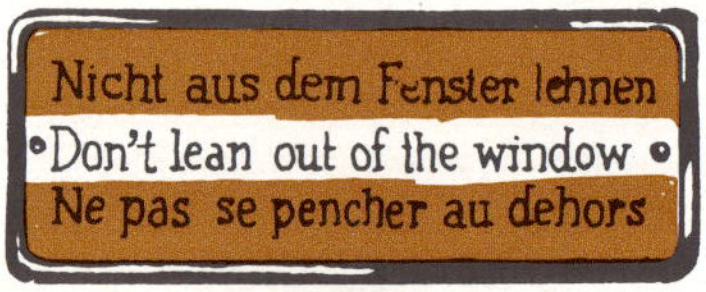

A 3

Home finding
1 Start here.
2
3 Your husband/wife is not at home. Don't leave the house. Miss one turn.
4
5 You see a friend in his car. Ask him to take you to the house. Move on to number 8.
6
7 Your friend tells you that there isn't a garden. Wait and think about it. Miss one turn.
8
9 Your friend says the house is too expensive. Don't listen to him. Move on to number 10.
10
11 You haven't got the address with you. Go back to number 2.
12
13 The address is wrong. Phone the newspaper for the right address. Miss two turns.
14
15 The owner of the house is not at home and you must wait for him. Miss one turn.
16
17
18 Don't wait here. Move on to number 20.
19
20
21
22
23
24 The owner tells you that the price of the house is £290, not £190 per week. Don't give up, start again.
25
To let

A 4

The Millers are looking for a new house. A friend of Mr Miller's knows a nice house for them in a suburb. The Millers have a lot of questions:

– Is there a	park bus stop station school supermarket post office swimming pool	near the house?
Are there a lot of	shops gardens . . .	

– Yes, there | is. / are.

No, there | isn't. / aren't.

Try to answer their questions.

Ask your neighbour about where he lives: – Is there . . . near your | house. / flat?

A 5

Listen, please

Which holiday flat is it?

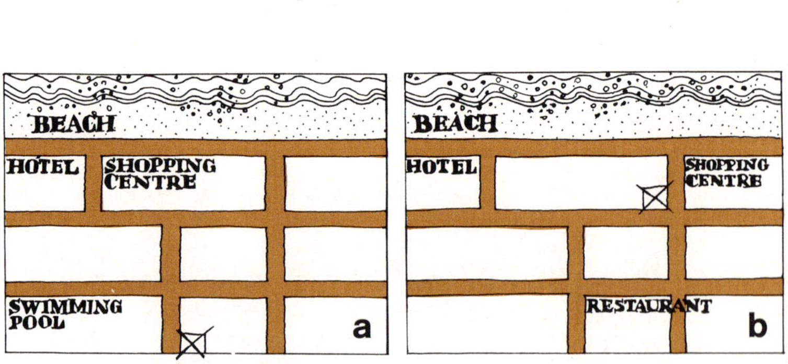

A 6 Do you get up early?

– Do you	get up early in the morning, Peter?	
	eat breakfast in a hurry?	
	travel to work by . . . ?	
	work in an office?	
	eat lunch in a canteen?	
	leave the office before 5 o'clock?	
	get home before your wife?	
	help . . . ?	– Yes, I do.
	. . . ?	No, I don't.

– Does your	wife	get up early in the morning?			
	son				
	friend		– Yes,	she	does.
	. . .			he	

► AB 2, AB 3, AB 7

A 7 The ideal husband or the ideal wife?

– Does your	husband	often	help you with the housework?
	wife	sometimes	stay at home when you can't find a baby-sitter?
			make you a cup of tea in the morning?
			buy you flowers?
			give you the keys to the car?
			meet you after night school?
			take you out?
			. . . ?

A 8 Do you like pop music?

– Do you like	pop music?		
	classical music?		
	modern art?		
	Westerns?		
	Italian food?	– Yes, I do.	Do you?
	French wine?	Not very much.	
	. . . ?	No, I don't.	

Ask your neighbour and then tell the group what he/she likes.

– Inge likes . . . , but she doesn't like . . . .

► AB 8

2 A 9 I like listening to music

– What do you do in your free time, Inge?

– I | listen to music.
go for a walk.
go to the theatre.
play tennis.
. . . .

– Do you like | listening to music, Peter?
going for a walk, . . . ?
playing tennis, . . . ?
. . . ing . . . ?

– Yes, I do.
No, I don't.

– What do you like doing in your free time?

– I | enjoy | playing the piano.
like | swimming.
. . . .

Ask your neighbour, and then tell the group what he/she likes doing in his/her free time.

– What does . . . like doing in her free time?

– He | likes . . . ing . . . .
She

– And what about your | husband?
wife?
. . . ?

► AB 5

A 10 Listen, please

a

Peter Howard
married, no children;
pop star; hobbies:
sport, modern art

b

Peter Johnson
married, 2 children;
actor; hobbies:
music, travelling

Who is the interviewer talking to?

A 11 My children don't watch TV all night

– What do young people do in their free time?

– They	spend a lot of money on	records. clothes. . . . .
	watch TV listen to pop music	all night.
	go to discos go to the cinema	every evening.
	. . . .	

– Do your children spend a lot of money on records, Inge?

– No, they don't spend a lot of money on records, but they spend a lot of money on books.

– Does your son/daughter watch TV all night, Peter?

– No, he/she doesn't watch TV, but he/she listens to pop music all night.

A 12 I think it's terrible

– I think it's terrible that so many young people | take drugs.
drink alcohol.
. . . .

– Yes, you're right, | but what can we do about it?
Yes, I agree it **is** terrible, |

– Parents can give their children more love.
Parents must talk to their children.
They must help them more with school problems.
They must try to understand them.
Parents must give a good example.
. . . .

► AB 9

3 **B**

POP STARS

– And now our special phone-in programme – today with Simon Hargreaves, Patti Miller, and Tony Terror.

Can we have the questions, please?

– Have you got a hobby?

– Yes, I have. I like playing tennis, but I haven't got a lot of time for my hobby.

– No, I haven't. Music is my job and my hobby.

– Yes, of course. But I can't tell you on the radio.

– Do you like classical music?

– Yes, I do. I often listen to good music. I sometimes get good ideas for my songs from classical music.

– Beethoven and that sort of thing? Look, man, my music **is** classical.

– I'm afraid I don't understand classical music.

– Some pop stars take drugs. Do you understand why?

– Yes, I do. They want to forget their problems. They think they can play better when they take drugs.

– Do you want to say that it's wrong to take drugs? Oh, come on, if a person enjoys it, why not . . . ?

– Well, I think so. A lot of people drink alcohol or eat a lot. That's a kind of drug, too, I think.

– Do you believe in what you sing?

– Yes, I do. I sing what I feel.

– What a question. Do you believe in what you do from nine to five?

– No, I don't. I sing what people want to hear. ►

– Do you enjoy singing?

– Never. It's a job.

– Yes, I do. I like singing, but the money is important, too.

– Ah, well, in show business you can't always do what you like.

– You must get a lot of money for concerts. Do you sometimes say no when people ask you to give a concert?

– Well, if it's in a small town like, like, – *er* – Manchester, I do. I always go to the big cities.

– No, I don't. I want to buy a hotel in Scotland.

– Yes, I do. Money isn't everything. Free time is important, too.

– Do you think your music is important?

– Yes, I do. I make people happy. When I sing they can forget their problems.

– No, I don't. I don't think show business is so important.

– Do you mean – like classical music? Of course it is.

– Are you happy with your kind of life?

– Oh yes, I am. I enjoy every minute of it.

– Sometimes I'm not. I don't like living out of a suitcase all the time.

– Well, it's not so bad, with all the money you can get, and all the girls.

► D 1, D 2, AB 1, AB 6

C1

Wait! – Don't cross now!

§ 21 ► D 3

C2 Yes/no-questions with do/does and short answers

– **Do** you smoke?	– Yes, **I** / **we** **do.**	– No, **I** / **we** **don't.**
– **Do** the Meiers smoke?	– Yes, **they do.**	– No, **they don't.**
– **Does** Peter / Susan smoke?	– Yes, **he** / **she** **does.**	– No, **he** / **she** **doesn't.**

If there **isn't** a word like **is, can, must, have,** you must use DO/DOES to make a question. (Questions with *is, can, must, have* → Units 1-5)

§§ 8, 18, (38, 39) ► AB 2, AB 3, D 5

C 3

I like pop music,	but	I **don't** like classical music.
Peter / Susan drink**s** wine,	but / but	he / she **doesn't** drink whisky.
We work on Friday,	but	we **don't** work on Saturday.
You speak German,	but	you **don't** speak French.
They read newspapers,	but	they **don't** read books.

If there **isn't** a word like **is, can, have** in the sentence, you must use DO/DOES to make a sentence with NOT.

	we write	*we say*
I you we they	do not	don't
he she it	does not	doesn't

§§ 12, (38, 39) ►D 4

C 4

Verb + -ing forms

Peter **likes listening** to pop music.
I **enjoy listening** to classical music.

(§ 220) ►AB 5

D 1

Interviewer

1 Does Simon/Patti/Tony believe in what he/she sings?

Manager or parents

a Yes, he does. He sings what he feels.

b No, she doesn't. She sings what people like to hear.

c . . . .

Go on with the questions and the answers.

4 **D 2**

Ask your neighbour about pop stars. Take the questions and answers from text B.

You

– Do you think pop stars like classical music?

Your neighbour

– Yes, I do. Sometimes they get good ideas for their songs from it.

D 3

Tony Terror's manager is talking to him.

Fill in don't *where you need it.*

1 ... stay up late when you have a concert the next day.
2 ... sing what people want to hear.
3 ... drink alcohol before a concert.
4 ... show people that you enjoy singing.
5 ... try to forget your problems when you sing.
6 ... spend so much money on girls.
7 ... forget that singing is your job.
8 ... listen to what I tell you.

D 4

Fill in the right form:
can't, doesn't/don't, hasn't got/haven't got.

1 Jim understands classical music but he ... understand modern music.

2 A lot of pop stars have only got time for their job, they ... time for their hobbies.

3 Ann knows a lot of good songs but she ... play them on the piano.

4 Fred thinks he can speak Italian but he ... understand everything when he is in Italy on holiday.

5 Tony drinks a lot but he ... take drugs.

6 The Millers have got a lot of money but they ... a lot of time for their children.

7 The keys must be in the living-room but I ... find them.

8 She has got a very good piano but she ... time to play it.

► AB 8

D 5

Ask the interviewer's questions:

1 have got/hobby ... ?
2 can speak/German ... ?
3 be happy/with your kind of life ... ?
4 your father/sometimes go to your concerts ... ?
5 have got/a lot of girlfriends ... ?
6 pop stars/can play better/take drugs ... ?
7 your mother/like/your music ... ?
8 your parents/be happy/about your job ... ?

► AB 4, AB 10

Unit 8 **Jobs**

A1 Young people and their jobs

Valerie is 20. She is a men's hairdresser. She is saving every penny, because she wants to open a hairdresser's shop one day. So her room in Wimbledon, a suburb of London, is full of old things from second-hand shops or from Portobello Road.

Peter, her boyfriend, is a student at London University. He still lives with his parents, who have a house in Richmond. Every morning he travels by Underground to the centre of London. After his exams he wants to marry Valerie if he can find a job as a teacher.

Susan, 19, is a secretary. She is not very happy about her job. She does not like her boss, her colleagues do not like her, and her wages are not very good. But it is difficult for her to find another job, because she lives in a village near Brighton and has a child of two. She is not married and has not got enough money for a baby-sitter. That is why she lives near her parents.

John is 18, and he is out of work again. He, too, lives with his parents in a flat in London near Holland Park. His father works in a factory, but John, who wants to work as a waiter, cannot find a job. John and his parents are from the West Indies.

►

What does Valerie do with her wages?
Where does she live?
Where does she buy things for her room?

Where does Peter study?
Where do his parents have a house?
What does he want to do after his exams?

Where does Susan live?
Why does she live near her parents?

Where do John's parents come from?
Where do they live at the moment?
Where does his father work?
Where does John want to work? ► AB 2

A 2

Where do you (does your girlfriend/boyfriend/...) live?
Where do you (does he/she) work?
How do you (does he/she) travel to work?
When do you (does he/she) get back in the evening?
What do you do when your husband is at work?
...? ► D 2

A 3

I'm not sure

– Why does Peter still live with his parents?
Why does Susan live near her parents, do you think?
Why does Susan still work in the same office?
Why do boys like John find it difficult to get a job?
Why do African students find it difficult to find rooms in London?
Why do so many Germans go to London for a weekend?
Why does the policeman ask Glenda Grey so many questions, do you think?
...?

– I'm not sure, but I think it's because she wants to ... .
Perhaps he wants ... .
I think it's because ... . ► AB 8

A 4

Do you remember the Broughtons on the strike day?
Ask your neighbours some questions.

Why doesn't Jim agree with his colleagues?
Why doesn't he speak to his wife?
Why doesn't Doris do the shopping in the afternoon?
...?

A 5 Listen, please

Who is it?

John Graham **a**	Bob Black **b**
Ladies' hairdresser	Men's hairdresser
Works in Central London	Works in Richmond
Travels to work by Underground	Travels to work by bus
Does not like his job	Likes his job

A 6 Why don't you ... ?

Susan – I'm so unhappy. I don't like my boss, and the wages are bad.
– Well, why don't you get another job?

John – I'd like to work as a waiter, but I can't find a job in London.
– Why ... ?

Peter – I can never go to a theatre with Valerie, because there are no late trains to Richmond.
– ... by car?

Fred Ferguson – I think Italy is too expensive for holidays.
– ... ?

Patti – I don't like living out of a suitcase all the time.
– ... ?

Tom Brown – It takes me two hours to get to work by car with all the traffic.
– ... ?

Glenda Grey – A man phones me every night at eleven o'clock.
– ... the police?

– ... .

► AB 4

A 7 Fred Mills has got a problem

He lives in a London suburb and works in the city centre.

If he drives to work it takes him 50 minutes, but it's difficult to find somewhere to park.

If he goes by train it takes him an hour, because it is a twenty-minute walk to the station.

If he goes by bus it takes him an hour and ten minutes, because he has to take three different buses.

And what about you?

– If I	drive to work go by train walk ...	it takes me ... .

► AB 5

A 8 Listen, please

How does he go to the airport?

a

b

c

A 9 Do you think it's fair?

Pat has a part-time job in a supermarket, but her husband never helps her with the housework. One day she says to him:

– When I make the breakfast, you read the morning paper.

When I do the washing-up in the evening, you watch TV.

When I work in the garden at the weekend, you listen to the sports news.

When I play with the children, you play tennis with Jill.

When I'm doing the housework, you're flirting with your secretary at the office.

Do you think it's fair?

If you don't help me with the housework, I can't work in the supermarket any more, and

if I don't work there any more, we cannot save for our holidays in Spain.

Oh, Fred, I really don't think it's fair.

– What does your husband do when you	do the housework? play with the children? . . . ?

– He	always . . .	helps me. . . . .

– What do you do when your wife	does the housework, Peter? . . . ?

– I often . . . .
I can never help her, because . . . .

– What a	wonderful terrible	husband	you've got! you are!

JOBS

4, Beech Grove,
Darlington,
Co. Durham.

21st October

Dear Cathy,

What a wonderful new job you've got. You really are lucky. You leave the house every day, work in a nice office and meet lots of interesting people.

But isn't it too much for you? When do you get up now? When do you do the shopping? When do you do all the housework? And when do you see Eric? Is he happy about the job?

Fred works for ICI now. He goes to Billingham every morning. He gets up very early and leaves the house before the children get up. He travels by train because it's safer in winter. He likes his job, but he often gets home late, and sometimes the children only see him at the weekends.

My life is just the same as before. Fred often says: "Why don't you look for a part-time job?" But I think that a part-time job *and* housework *and* a family is too much for me. Everything is different if you have children.

Well, I must stop now - the children are in the bath and it's their bedtime.

I hope to hear from you soon.

Love,

Jean

12, Gledhow Valley Road,
Leeds 17,
LS17 1HN

28th October

Dear Jean,

Thank you very much for your letter, Eric is happy about my new job. Why do you ask? The job isn't too bad, you know, but it isn't so interesting. After all, what do you do in an office? You type letters and answer phone calls all day. Most of the time I only see my boss - his name is Martin - and he's the sales manager - but you can't say that he's very interesting.

Sometimes I think that a housewife's life isn't so bad. If you have a job you're always in a hurry. I usually get up at half past six, and I do most of the housework in the evening. There's never enough time for the shopping. I go shopping at the weekend, and you know that most things are very expensive then.

It's not so much the money that's important, you know. I work for things like the car and the new TV, of course, but Eric drives the car most of the time, and he watches TV when I do the washing-up. - Well, he helps sometimes.

But it's a change to get out of the house. You say Fred gets home late. When does he get back in the evening? And what does he do then? (By the way, why does he work for ICI now? Are the wages better there?) Eric is always tired after work, and he doesn't talk very much in the evening. And what does Fred do at the weekend? For Eric it's only the car and football. It's the same old story. What do you do all day when Fred is away? Why don't you try a part-time job?

Well, that's all for now. Love to Fred and the children.

Your loving sister,

Cathy

► D 1, AB 1, AB 6, AB 7

C 1 Questions

						→ Unit
I Yes/no-questions		Is	John		an actor?	1
		Are	there		two bathrooms?	2
		Can	you	get	stamps there?	3
		Have	you	got	a car?	4
		Is	Jim	talking	to his wife?	5
		Do	you	travel	to work by bus?	7
		Does	your husband	help	you?	
II W-questions	Where	is	Carl Wagner		from?	1
	What	must	a secretary	do	in your office?	3
	What	are	you	doing?		5
	When	**do**	you	have	lunch on Sundays?	6/8
	How	**do**	you	like	your colleagues?	
	When	**does**	he	get up	in the morning?	
	Why	**does**	Glenda Grey	phone	the police?	
	What	**does**	John	think	of him?	
	...	**...**	...	...	...?	

In these questions there is always a word like **is, can, must, have** at the beginning or after the question word. If there isn't, you must use DO/DOES.

§§ 7–10 ►D 2, D 4, D 5

C 2

Susan – I don't like my job.
Friend – Why don't you get another job?

Stan Why aren't you picketing?

Cindy – Why aren't you working then?

Questions like these are not always real questions. They often mean something else, for example

- that you want to tell a person what to do,
- that you disagree,
- that you don't understand *why* a person does what he does.

§§ 13–16 ►AB 4

C 3 Why?

I'm speaking English **because** he can't speak German.
He can't speak German. | **That's why** / **So** | I'm speaking English.

C 4

	1	2		3	4	
If	I	leave	the house at 7,	I	get	to the office at 8.
If	Jim	is	on strike,	his wife	gets	less money.

	1		2	4	3	
Wenn	*ich*	*das Haus um 7 Uhr*	*verlasse,*	*komme*	*ich*	*um 8 ins Büro.*
Wenn	*Jim*		*streikt,*	*bekommt*	*seine Frau*	*weniger Geld.*

► D 3

C 5

He **doesn't know**	how	to	get there.
	where	to	park.
	what	to	do.
	wh...	to	....

C 6

It's	too	expensive.
	too	much.
	too	....

(§ 205)

D 1 **Some questions about the story**

Where does Jean's husband work?
When does he get up?
When does he leave the house?
How does he travel to work?
When do the children see him?
Why doesn't Jean look for a part-time job?
What does she think of Cathy's new job?

What does Cathy think of her job?
What does she do at the office?
When does she get up?
Why does she work in the office?
What does Eric do to help her?
... ?

D 2 *Ask your neighbour*

- if she/he likes living in.... .
- when she/he gets up in the morning.
- who gets up first, she/he or her husband/his wife.
- who makes the breakfast.
- who leaves the house first in the morning, she/he or her husband/his wife.
- how many rooms she/he has got in her/his flat.
- what car she/he drives.
- if she/he likes the night school class.
- if she/he often has a drink after class.
- when she/he gets home after class.
- ....

Can you think of any more questions?

► AB 2

D 3

Dear Abby,

I often feel that a housewife's "job" isn't really important. My husband has a very good job, and I don't need to work because there is enough money, but he often says: "Why don't you work in the mornings like your sister?" But I think that if a woman has a part-time job,

she	can't play with her children so often. can't do so much work in the house and in the garden. hasn't got enough time for her husband/children/hobbies. often has to pay a lot of money for a baby-sitter. has to do the shopping when the shops are full. often does the housework on Sunday when her husband is at home. . . . .

That's why I don't want to work in an office or in a shop. But my husband says: "If you only do housework all day, what can we talk about in the evening?" Who is right – my husband or me? Can you please help me?

Yours,

Ann S.

Dear Ann S.,

A lot of women have the same problem. Of course they can't ..., if they ... . And they haven't got ..., if they ... . But, then, think of the time when you are older and the children are out of the house.
If a woman spends all her time in the house,

she	doesn't meet so many interesting people. doesn't have money of her own. doesn't feel as important as other women who go out to work.

So why don't you ... ?

► AB 5

Yours, Abby

D 4 Mr Miller is at the doctor's. He works very hard and finds it difficult to sleep at night. The doctor has a lot of questions.

Doctor	**Mr Miller**
Do you drink a lot of coffee?	No, I only drink tea.
How many cups of tea ... ?	Well, two or three in the morning, and three or four in the afternoon.
... smoke?	Yes, I do.
... ?	Oh, about 30 cigarettes a day, I think.
... alcohol?	Sometimes, but not very much.
When ... ?	I usually get up at six.
Why ... so early?	There a lot of things to do in the house before I leave.
... work?	In Birmingham, 8 miles from here.
When ... ?	Oh, very late. I leave the office at about 6, but I never get home before 7.
Why ... ?	I often have a drink with my friends before I go home.
What ... ?	I sometimes watch TV, but I often take work home.
When ... ?	Never before 11.30.

▸ AB 3

D 5 Are these questions about
a you,
b your neighbour(s),
c a book?

1 Does your hobby sometimes help you to be happy?
2 Do you live here?
3 Is it on your desk?
4 Does he work near here?
5 Does she like your house?
6 What does it say about houses in Spain?
7 Do you like Patrick Mulligan?
8 Is it difficult to get?
9 Can they tell him where he can get jeans?
10 Why do you read that newspaper?

Unit 9 Holidays – a change?

A1 What did Linda do yesterday?

She got up at 7.45.

She ate her breakfast in a hurry.

She left the house at 8.15.

She took the 8.20 bus to the office.

She started work at 8.45.

She typed a lot of letters and made phone calls.

She had a tea-break at 9.45.

She left the office at 12.45.

In the afternoon
Linda read a book.

She listened to the radio.

She drank a cup of tea.

In the evening
she met her friends and
went to the cinema.

– What did she do | at … ?
in … ?

A 2 And how did Martha spend her day?

1
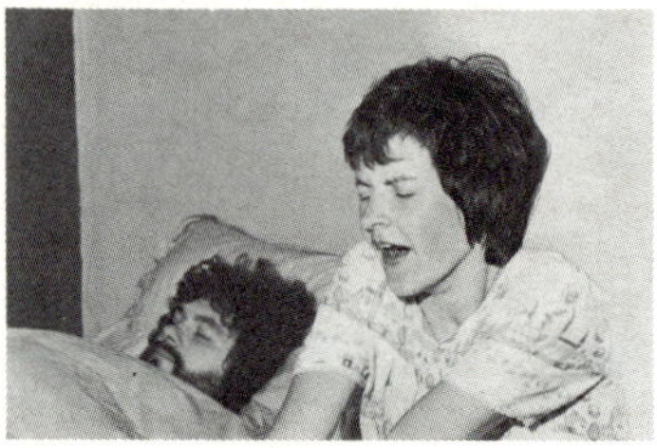
She got up at 7.

2

She made breakfast for the family at 7.30.

3
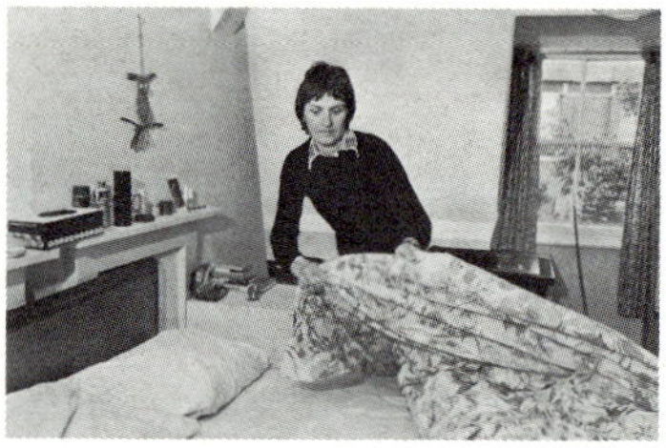
She made the beds at 9.

4

She worked in the garden from 9.30 to 10.

5

She went shopping at 10.

6

She did the washing-up at 12.

7

In the afternoon she played with the children.

8

In the evening she watched TV with her husband.

– What did she do	at ... ?		– At ...	she ....
	in ... ?		In ...	

► D 4, AB 4

A 3 When did your parents get a TV?

– When did	you your parents	get	a TV? a car? a film camera? a radio? a telephone? central heating? hot water? a toilet inside the flat? . . . ?

– About . . . years ago.
I think it was in 1920.
I'm not sure, but I think . . . .
I'm afraid I don't know.
I'm afraid I can't remember.

► AB 5

A 4 Where did you live when you were 16?

– Did you	smoke always do what your parents told you still go to school like classical music have a boyfriend/girlfriend already know your husband/wife . . .	when you were 16?

– Yes, I did.
No, I didn't.
I'm afraid I can't remember.

► D 5

A 5

Nice day today

– Good morning.

– Morning. What a beautiful morning!

– Yes, wonderful. Real holiday weather.

– Hmm, we're lucky. Have a nice day!

Terrible weather!

– Morning.

– Morning. Terrible weather!

– Yes, it is. It *always* is at the weekend.

– Just when I wanted to work in the garden!

A 6 Yesterday's weather

– What was the weather like in . . . yesterday?

– It was . . . .

– What was the weather like when you were on holiday?

YESTERDAY'S WEATHER

	°C	
ATHENS	28	sunny
BARCELONA	20	cloudy
BIARRITZ	21	stormy
CAIRO	31	hot, dry
COLOGNE	15	cool
DUBLIN	10	cold, rain

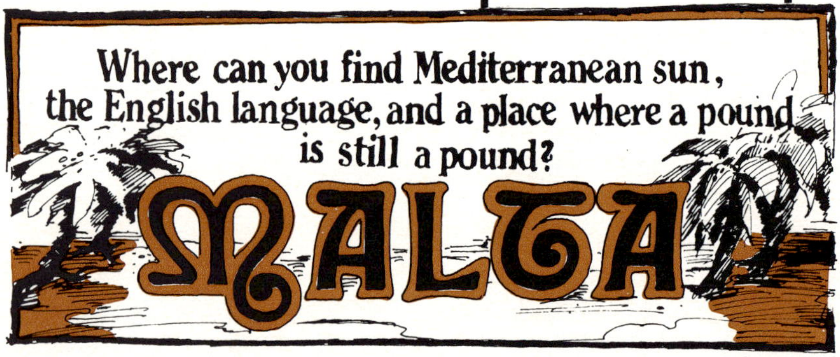

► AB 9

A 7 Listen, please

Today's weather in the London area.

A 8 What did you do during your last holiday?

– Last summer	I	went to . . . .
Two years ago	we	spent our holidays in . . . .
		stayed in . . . .

– When the weather was fine	I we	did a lot of sight-seeing. lay in the sun all day. made trips to . . . . played . . . . swam a lot. . . . .
When it was bad		played cards. watched TV. . . . .

▸ AB 3

A 9 Did you enjoy your holidays?

– I liked the	place, people, sun, group, hotel, . . . ,	but I didn't like the	flat/hotel. food. beach. tour guide. manager. . . . .

▸ AB 2

A 10 Where did you stay?

– Where did you stay during your last holidays? In a hotel, in a holiday flat, or did you go camping?

– We stayed in a . . . .
We went camping.

– Did you have to | make the beds every morning?
do all the cooking?
go shopping every day?
clear it up when you left?

– Yes, we did.
No, we didn't, but we had to . . . .

► AB 6

A 11 Listen, please

1
Where did Charles spend his holidays?

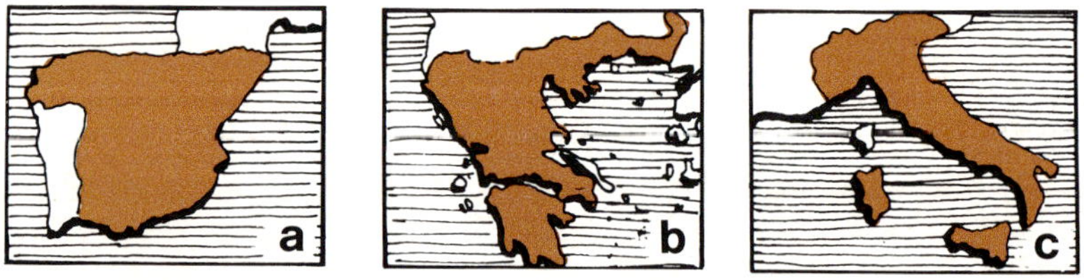

2
Where did he stay?

3
What was the weather like?

Notes

B

2

A Busman's Holiday

1979

June

WEEK 24

17 Sat
10 a.m. We got up at 5 o'clock to be at the airport for 9 o'clock, when the plane leaves for RIMINI! I'm really looking forward to two weeks in the sun. A real holiday at last!

18 Sun
11 a.m. The plane was late. We arrived in Rimini at 2 o'clock in the morning! The holiday flat is nice, but not very clean. If the children help me, we can go out for lunch at 1.

19 Mon
We all had pizza last night – and Fred and I had wine. Fred liked the wine, but the wine did not like him. He got up at 2 o'clock in the afternoon, so today I did the washing-up and made the beds. Alison and John played with the neighbours' children – they are from Birmingham.

20 Tue
I did not sleep all night. The disco under the flat was open till 3 o'clock – and they said at the travel agency that it was a quiet flat! Fred slept until lunchtime again and I did all the housework again. It's not different from life at home. The children were out all day, of course.

21 Wed
Fred came back with that woman from Birmingham last night. I went out and didn't get back until two in the morning. I met Mario at the disco. Was it the wine, or was it ...?

22 Thu
He did not get up at all today! I went swimming with the children in the morning, did the housework and shopping in the afternoon and spoke to the travel agent.
Fred was fine in the evening, and went out with the other men.

23 Fri
Fred did not come home at all last night. The children were sweet. When they saw I was unhappy they made a cup of coffee and helped me to make the breakfast. I didn't speak a word to him all day. We can't go on like this. Tomorrow ...

►

– Did you have a nice holiday, Fred?

– It wasn't bad, thanks.

– Did Pat enjoy it?

– Yes, I think so. She didn't say much, but I think she had a good time.

– What was the flat like?

– Oh, it wasn't too bad. It's not like in England, of course. We had to clear it up a bit at first. But it was no problem after that.

– What was the place like? Were there a lot of things to do – pubs, discos?

– Well, we didn't go out much. Pat didn't like the Italians very much. We met some very nice people from Birmingham. The wife was very understanding. A really nice woman. He was a bit quiet. Funny, Pat didn't like them very much.

– By the way, Margaret told me that Pat is staying with her mother at the moment.

– Yes, her mother's not very well. Well, I really must stop now, Bill. I've to make tea for Alison and John. Goodbye.

– Oh, goodbye, Fred. And give my best wishes to Pat.

► D 1, AB 1, AB 7

C 1 THE SIMPLE PAST, regular form

I	**worked**	on Saturday.	I	**didn't work**	on Sunday.
You	**typed**	a story last night.	You	**didn't type**	a letter.
John	**played**	table tennis yesterday.	He	**didn't play**	tennis.
Mary	**watched**	'Bonanza' that evening.	She	**didn't watch**	Liza Minelli.
We	**liked**	our hotel.	We	**didn't like**	the food there.
They	**closed**	the door this morning, but	they	**didn't close**	the window.

answer ed listen ed play ed rain ed . . .	wa shed wat ched ty ped . . .	want ed . . .
[d]	[t] *after* [f], [k], [p], [s], [ʃ]	[id] *after* t, d

§§ 54–56

C 2 **Yes/no-questions and short answers**

– **Did** you **play** tennis yesterday? – Yes, I **did.**

– **Did** he **play** tennis yesterday? – No, he **didn't.**

(§§ 8, 18, 39)

C 3 W-questions

– What **did** you **do** last night?	– I typed the letter.
– When **did** she **type** the letter?	– She typed it last night.

(§§ 10, 39)

C 4 Some irregular forms

I begin,	I began [bɪ'gæn]	I mean,	I meant [ment]
I buy,	I bought [bɔ:t]	I meet,	I met [met]
I come,	I came [keɪm]	I read [ri:d],	I read [red]
I do,	I did [dɪd]	I say [seɪ],	I said [sed]
I drink,	I drank [dræŋk]	I sell,	I sold [səʊld]
I drive,	I drove [drəʊv]	I sing,	I sang [sæŋ]
I eat,	I ate [et]	I sit,	I sat [sæt]
I feel,	I felt [felt]	I sleep,	I slept [slept]
I forget,	I forgot [fə'gɒt]	I speak,	I spoke [spəʊk]
I get,	I got [gɒt]	I spend,	I spent [spent]
I give,	I gave [geɪv]	I stand,	I stood [stʊd]
I go,	I went [went]	I swim,	I swam [swæm]
I hear,	I heard [hɜ:d]	I take,	I took [tʊk]
I know,	I knew [nju:]	I tell,	I told [təʊld]
I leave,	I left [left]	I think,	I thought [θɔ:t]
I lie,	I lay [leɪ]	I win,	I won [wʌn]
I make,	I made [meɪd]	I write,	I wrote [rəʊt]

§ 54

C 5 Some more irregular forms

I have(n't)	– I **had**(n't)	I am/I'm not	– I **was**(n't)
		you are(n't)	– you **were**(n't)
he has(n't)	– he **had**(n't)	he/she/it is(n't)	– he/she/it **was**(n't)
we have(n't)	– we **had**(n't)	we/you/they are(n't)	– we/you/they **were**(n't)

§§ 28, 33 ►D 2, D 3, D 4, D 5, AB 2

C 6 MUST/HAVE TO – HAD TO

I **must** / **have to** get up at 6 every morning.	(SIMPLE PRESENT)
I **had to** get up at 5 yesterday.	(SIMPLE PAST)
Did you **have to** get up early for the bus? **Do** you **have to** get up early every morning?	**(Questions)**

§ 75 ►AB 6

3 D1

Some questions on the text. Give short answers.

1 ... they ... (get up) very early when they went on holiday?	– Yes, they ....
2 ... (be) the plane late?	– ..., ...
3 ... they only ... (eat) English food in Rimini?	– ..., ...
4 ... Fred ... (drink) a lot of wine during his holidays?	– ..., ...
5 ... Fred always ... (go) to bed early?	– ..., ...
6 ... Pat ... (like) Mario?	– ..., ...
7 ... (be) there a lot to do in Rimini?	– ..., ...
8 ... they ... (have) a lot of problems during their holidays?	– ..., ...

D2

Fill in the past tense of these verbs:

buy – be – go – have – drink – eat – leave – take – get – sing

1 Last week I ... a new car.
2 I ... very happy when I ... to town to get it.
3 I remember that I was in such a hurry that I ... only half my breakfast.
4 I only ... a cup of coffee and ... one piece of toast.
5 I ... the house and ... the next bus into town.
6 I was so happy when I ... my new car that I ... all the way home.

► AB 3

D3

Pop stars

Some pop stars finish their career because ...

1 they are too old.
2 people don't want to see them any more.
3 they begin to feel different about their music.
4 they think that their kind of life isn't interesting any more.
5 they want to do something else.
6 other pop stars leave the group.
7 they want to spend more time with their families.
8 ....

Interviewer		**Ex pop star**
– Why did you finish your career,	Eric? Graham? ...?	– I finished it because ....

► AB 5

D 4 What did Martha do yesterday?

What did she do first – then – after that – and then?	go shopping. have lunch. make breakfast. do the washing-up.	**first** ↓
What did Martha do in the afternoon and in the evening?	watch TV with her husband. play with her children. go to bed. have dinner.	**then** ↓
What did Linda do yesterday?	take the bus to the office. eat her breakfast in a hurry. leave the office at 12.45. type letters and make a lot of phone calls.	**after that** ↓
What did Linda do yesterday afternoon?	go to the cinema. read a book. listen to the radio. drink a cup of tea.	**and then**

► AB 4

D 5 *Can you answer these questions about the strike day?*

1 Did Jim Broughton go to work as usual? – No, he didn't. He stayed at home.
2 Did Cindy get to the office at 9? – No, she didn't. She got there at . . . .

Find more questions and ask your neighbour.

3 . . . go shopping . . . ? – . . . .
4 . . . agree with this strike? – No, ... He only . . . at home because he didn't want to . . . .
5 . . . picket . . . ? – . . . worked in the . . . .
6 . . . drive to work in her mother's car? – . . . drove . . . .

D 6 *Write a letter to an English friend about your last holiday.*

Remember to answer the following questions:
1 Where did you go?
2 How did you get there?
3 Where did you stay?
4 What did you do?
5 What was the weather like?

Food and drink

A1

Breakfast

Fruit Juice

Cornflakes

Bacon and Eggs

Toast or Brown Bread
Butter and Jam

Tea or Coffee

What would you like for breakfast?

– Good morning, Mr Philips. Did you sleep well?

– Yes, thank you, Mrs Brown.

– What would you like for breakfast?

– Have you got any orange juice?

– Yes, and what would you like to eat?

– I'd like some cornflakes, and bacon and eggs.

– Coffee or tea?

– Tea, please.

– When do you have breakfast?
– What do you usually have for breakfast?

A 2

Can I have the menu, please?

– What would you like to start with?

– I'd like . . . , please.

– And what would you like to follow?

– I'd like . . . with . . . .

– Would you like fruit or ice-cream?

– What's the fruit?

– Apples or pears.

– I'd like the ice-cream, please.

– Any drinks, sir/madam?

– Have you got . . . ?

– Yes, sir/madam.

– Thank you, that's all.

A 3 Bad luck!

Customer – I'd like tomato soup, please.
Waiter – Sorry, we haven't got any tomato soup.
Would you like some orange juice instead?

Angus steak/roast chicken chips/boiled potatoes salad/vegetables ice-cream/fruit coffee/tea

Customer – Can I have the bill, please?
Waiter – You had the businessman's lunch, and a glass of white wine.
That's £4.15, sir.
Customer – Oh, sorry. I haven't got any change.
Would you change this £20 note, please?
Waiter – I'm sorry, I can't.
Customer – Can I pay by cheque?
Waiter – Yes, of course, if you've got a cheque card.

A 4 Listen, please

What did they eat?

a	b	c
Tomato soup Roast chicken and chips Fruit Coffee	Fruit juice Angus steak and chips Fruit Coffee	Tomato soup Roast chicken boiled potatoes Ice-cream Tea

A 5 Let's have a party!

– What do we need for the party?

– We need some . . . .
Let's get / buy some . . . .

Write down your shopping lists in groups, then ask the other groups what they have got on their shopping lists:

– Have you got any / Is there any . . . on your list?

– Yes, there is.
No, there isn't. You're right, we need some . . . . / We don't need any . . . .

2 A 6 No, I'm afraid not

– Would you like some more | beer? / wine? / whisky?

– No, thank you. I'm afraid not. | I have to drive home. / I've got the car with me. | Have you got any orange juic

– Have you got some more	beer?	
	of that	red wine? Scotch whisky? nice salad?

– No, I'm afraid not, but I've got some . . . . Would you like some?

– Yes, please.
No, thanks. I don't like . . . .

► D 5, D 6, AB 2, AB 3

A 7 Are there any good restaurants here?

– Are there any good restaurants in . . . ?

– No, there aren't, but	there are some in . . . . there is one in . . . .
Yes, there are, there's	

– Which restaurant is | better, / bigger, | . . . or . . . ?

– I think . . . is | better / . . . | than . . . .

– Well, I think the food is better at . . . , but . . . is cheaper.

– Yes, but . . . is nicer.

– I'm afraid I don't agree,	I think I don't think	. . . is as	good . . .	as . . . .

A 8 Are things really cheaper in England?

– Is wine		cheaper more expensive	in	England Spain Italy	than in Germany?
Are	cigarettes clothes hotels ...				

– Yes,	it is. they are.
I really don't know. I'm not sure, but I think	
No,	it isn't. It's cheaper in .... they aren't. They're cheaper in ....

▸ D 3

A 9 Which is cheaper?

You are travelling by | car. / train.

Where would you like to stay

a for one night?

b for 6 nights?

c if you don't want to spend a lot of money?

HENLEY-ON-THAMES Map 7 B
Oxon
Hotels
**** **Caversham Bridge** Caversham
T 53631 80 rms private bathrooms
bar TV tennis 25 min from centre
very quiet
*** **Great Western** Station Rd
T 52355 200 rms bathrooms on all
floors 3 min from station
* **King's Head** London Rd (A 14)
T 52195 12 rms fully licensed TV
garage
Daisy Banks B&B Park Street
T 41732 3 rms

Which hotel is | cheaper? / more expensive? / quieter? / more comfortable? / nearer to the | town centre? / station? / bigger? / nicer? / better? / ...?

I think	the ... Daisy Banks	is	more expensive than the .... cheaper than the ....
			as nice as the .... not as nice as the ....

▸ AB 5

A 10 It's the best hotel in town

– I'm looking for a	good cheap quiet comfortable	hotel. Can you help me, please?

– Well,	there's the try the	Milton. Bären.	It's the	best cheapest quietest most comfortable	hotel in town.

But it's also the most expensive.

▶ D 4, AB 4, AB 6

A 11 Listen, please

DENFORD Map 5 A
Wessex
Hotels
**** **The Russell** Forest Road
T 532 873 125 rms private bathrooms
bar TV tennis swimming pool
15 min from centre very quiet
£40-£60 breakfast extra
** **The George** Poplar Drive
T 502 337 75 rms fully licensed
bathrooms on all floors bar TV
garage £15-£35 B&B
* **The Railway** Station Square
T 521 533 30 rms bathrooms on all
floors TV 2 min from station
£10-£18 B&B

Which hotel do they want to go to?

a The Russell Hotel

b The George Hotel

c The Railway Hotel

A 12 Listen, please

The restaurant he is talking about is

1	a Chinese	b English	c Indian

and is in

2	a North Street	b Baker Street	c George Street

A 13

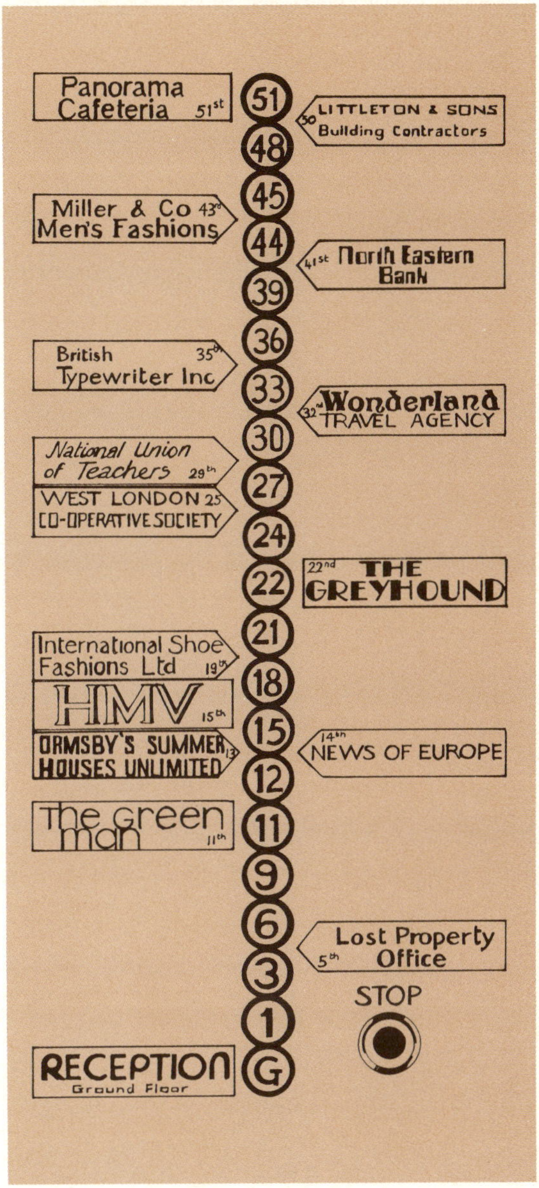

This is the lift in the office building where Fred Mills works.

It stops only at every third floor.

It also stops at the 11th and the 22nd floor because there are snack-bars on those floors.

There are a lot of offices in the building. The man at the reception can tell you how to get there.

Ask him.

– Excuse me, I'm looking for . . . .
which floor is . . . on?
on which floor can I find . . . ?

– They're on the . . . floor. You can take the lift to the . . . floor. Then you must walk upstairs/downstairs.

Eati
in London

A lot of tourists have the same problem when they are in London: where to eat lunch. Some, of course, have enough money to eat in one of the more expensive hotels or restaurants in the West End. But most of them just want to sit in a quiet place, get a good meal, and they don't want to pay too much for it. This kind of place is not easy to find.

The best restaurants are, of course, as comfortable as most of the better restaurants in Germany or in France, but they are also as expensive, and some people say that the food is not as good as, for example, in a much cheaper restaurant in France.

In the less expensive places the food is as 'American' as in all international snack-bars. You can go to a WIMPY Bar in London, in New York or wherever you like in the world and have a hamburger, a cheeseburger or some other kind of -burger there. This is what most Londoners do, if they work in the City and cannot go home for lunch. In the self-service restaurants in the department stores you can get fish and chips or some other "delicacy", like bacon and eggs. But, although the food is a lot cheaper there than in a good hotel, many foreigners say that they do not really like it.

Most of these restaurants are not fully licensed, and this is important if you like a glass of be with your lunch, because you ca not get any alcoholic drinks ther If the drink is more important tc you than the food, you can, of course, go to a pub and eat a sar wich there and drink a glass of beer. And more and more pubs are now offering lunch.

Out

ᶠ pub food is not quite what you ‹e, there are also a lot of foreign estaurants in London. In Soho ıere are hundreds of them, and ome of them are really nice. here are some Indian or Pakistani estaurants where food is cheaper ıan in other restaurants. The pizza ı some of the Italian restaurants an be as good as pizza in Italy ınd sometimes even better). And, ᶠ you like Chinese food, you can lways try one of the Chinese estaurants. But look at the menu

first, because some of these places, for example in Chelsea, are getting more expensive every day.

Why are most of these Indian and Chinese restaurants a lot cheaper than other restaurants? The reason is that a lot of people from Commonwealth countries who live in London often work there for less money than the British, because they cannot find better jobs.

But where can you find 'typically English' food in London? After all, most people do not travel to London to eat pizza! Well, you can, of course, live with an English family for some time, and find that food in England is not as bad as most people say.

Adapted from: 'Eating Out in London', Gourmet Publications, London 1978, pp 3-5

► D 1, AB 1, AB 7

C1

WOULD LIKE

I'd **like**	**a cup** of coffee, please.	(= I **would like**)
	to go to the cinema tonight.	

Yes/no-questions and short answers

Would you **like** some tea?	– Yes, please. No, thank you.
Would you **like** to go to the cinema?	– Yes, that's a good idea. No, I'm afraid I haven't got any time.
Would you **like** tea or coffee?	– Tea, please.

W-questions

What **would** you **like**	for breakfast?
	to follow?

§§ 78, 79

C2

SOME	NOT . . . ANY
Mr Smith wants to buy **some** cigarettes.	He has**n't** got **any** cigarettes.
There are **some** cigarettes over there on the table.	I ca**n't** find **any** cigarettes.
I'd like **some** French cigarettes, please.	I'm sorry, we have**n't** got **any**.

If there is NOT in the sentence, you must use ANY.

§§ 140, 141 ►D 5

C3

Have you got **any**	coffee?
	pears?

Can I have **some**	coffee,	please?
	pears,	

In questions you must use →

ANY	if the ANSWER can be YES or NO,
SOME	if you think that the ANSWER is YES.

§§ 140, 141 ►D 6

C4

everybody	everyone	everything	everywhere
somebody	someone	. . .	. . .
anybody	any. . .	. . .	. . .
nobody	no-one	. . . [ˈnʌθɪŋ]	. . .

Can you go on? C 2 *and* C 3 *tell you how to use these words.* §§ 142–146, 149, 150

C 5 Comparisons

I	Peter is **as** old **as** Jim. Jim is **not as** old **as** Frank. Hotels in England are **as** expensive **as** hotels in Germany. German films are **not as** interesting **as** Italian films.
II	Frank is old**er than** Peter. The pizza at Gino's is **better than** at Mario's. A Rolls-Royce is **more** expensive **than** a Mini.
III	Frank is **the** old**est** student in our class. 'The Burglar' is **the most** interesting story in our English book.

I	. . . **as** + *old* + **as** . . . . . . **not as** + *old* + **as** . . .
II	short words: *old* + **-er** + **than** long words: **more** + *expensive* + **than**
III	short words: *old* + **-est** long words: **most** + *interesting*

Irregular:			
	good	better	best
	a lot of	more	most

§§ 172–178 ▶D 2, D 3, D 4

D 1 Right or wrong?

1 Most tourists in London eat in expensive restaurants.

2 The best restaurants in London are not as comfortable as the better restaurants in France and Germany.

3 Food in the snack-bars of the department stores is cheaper.

4 In most English snack-bars you cannot get any alcohol.

5 Foreign restaurants in London are usually more expensive than English restaurants.

6 Some Chinese restaurants are getting more expensive every day.

D 2

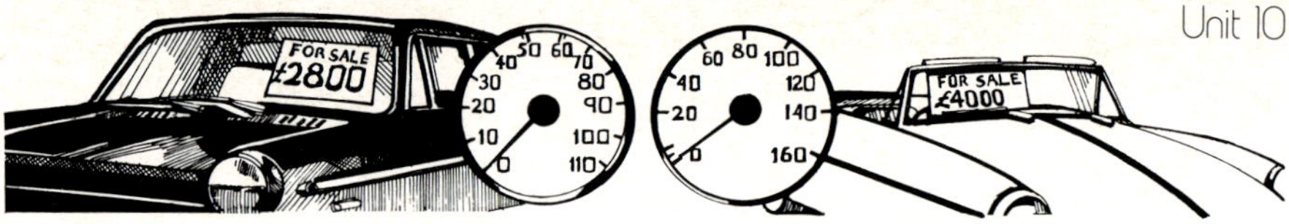

The car salesman wants to sell the sports car to Mr Brown, but Mr Brown thinks that the family car is better for him. What do they say about the two cars?

Salesman – This sports car is the car for you. It's much . . . than the family car. (fast)

Mr Brown – Of course, the family car isn't . . . fast . . . the sports car, but it's . . . the sports car. (cheap)

Salesman – Yes, it's true that the sports car is . . . expensive . . . the family car, but the engine is . . . that of the family car. (big)

Mr Brown – That's right, the family car's engine isn't . . . big . . . that of the sports car, but it's . . . comfortable . . . the sports car.

Salesman – But don't you agree that the sports car is a very good car? It's the . . . car we have.

Mr Brown – Yes, but I think the family car is . . . for me . . . the sports car. (good)

► AB 4

D 3 **What do you think?**

– I think that apples are more expensive than pears at the moment.

– I don't agree. I don't think that apples are as expensive as pears.

1 a Mini/a Rabbit/comfortable
2 the tower of Pisa/St. Marks/interesting
3 cars in America/cars in Germany/modern
4 a happy life/a lot of money/important

► AB 5

4 ## D 4 *Use these words:*

comfortable – good – expensive – near – big

1 – Which is the cheapest supermarket in town? – The Co-op, I think.
2 – Which is . . . hotel in Henley? – The Caversham, I think.
3 – Which is . . . book shop in town? – Miller's, I'd say.
4 – Where is . . . post office? – In George Street.
5 – Which is . . . department store in town? – Binn's, I think.

► AB 6

D 5 **Some** or **any**?

1 – I'd like . . . Bourbon, please.
– Sorry, we haven't got . . . . But what about . . . . Scotch?

2 – There must be . . . cigarettes in this room.
– Sorry, but I can't find . . . .

3 – I'd like to buy . . . flowers for Mary, but I haven't got . . . money.

4 – If you can't get . . . blouses at Eve's, go to Gucci's. They have . . . very nice blouses there, but they are very expensive.

► AB 2

D 6 **Some** or **any**?

1

– Would you like . . . more tea?

2

– Are there . . . newspapers today?

3

– Can I have . . . pears, please?

4

– Have you got . . . pears today?

5

– Have you got . . . Italian wine, please?

► AB 3

6

– I'm sorry we haven't got any Irish whiskey. Would you like . . . Scotch instead?

D 7

Your friend wants to spend a long weekend in your home town and is looking for a hotel. There are two good hotels in your town. Write your friend a letter and tell him which hotel you think is better and why.

Wörterverzeichnis

Dieses Wörterverzeichnis ist als „Lernwörterbuch" angelegt: in der mittleren Spalte werden einsprachige Lernhilfen gegeben, die das Erschließen und Behalten der Wortbedeutung erleichtern sollen. Dabei werden nur jeweils bekannte Wörter und Strukturen verwendet; auf bedeutungsähnliche Wörter wird mit ≈ (‚ist ungefähr gleich') hingewiesen (z.B. fine ≈ nice), auf Wörter mit abweichender Bedeutung mit ≠ (‚ungleich'), (z.B. woman ≠ wife ≠ lady). Der Pfeil (→) verweist auf bereits früher vorgekommene andere oder ähnliche Bedeutungen; mit *opposite:* wird auf Gegensätze hingewiesen.

Sie arbeiten mit diesem Vokabelteil am besten wie folgt:

(1) Prägen Sie sich das neue Wort, die Beispiele oder Erklärungen in der mittleren Spalte und die Übersetzung zunächst gut ein.
(2) Decken Sie dann die linke Spalte mit den englischen Wörtern ab und versuchen Sie, in der mittleren Spalte das durch die Tilde (~) ersetzte Wort zu ergänzen; seine deutsche Übersetzung in der rechten Spalte kann Ihnen dabei als Erinnerungsstütze dienen. (Wenn diese Tilde am Anfang eines Satzes steht, findet sich davor *der erste Buchstabe* des Ausdrucks groß geschrieben, z.B. **of course** links, O~ I can. in der Mitte. Beachten Sie auch, daß bei Verben, die links in der Grundform mit *to* aufgeführt sind, *nur das Verb, nicht aber ‚to'* eingesetzt wird.)
(3) Wenn in der mittleren Spalte nichts steht, versuchen Sie, die deutsche Übersetzung mit dem in dieser Übung eingeführten Ausdruck wiederzugeben.

Wörter in **Fettdruck** sind im Zertifikatswortschatz des Deutschen Volkshochschulverbandes enthalten. Wörter in normalem Druck sind von solchen Wörtern abgeleitet und können daher auch Gegenstand der Zertifikatsprüfung sein. Erläuterte Sätze erscheinen in normaler Schrift. *Kursiv* gedruckte Wörter gehören zum lehrwerkspezifischen Wortschatz.

Zahlen → 2/C6, 3/C10, 4/C7; **Wochentage** → 4/C5; **Monatsnamen** → 4/C6.

Eine Übersicht der verwendeten **Lautschriftzeichen** befindet sich auf Seite 149. Auf Wörter, die oft falsch ausgesprochen werden, wird mit **[!]** hingewiesen. Bei diesen Wörtern sollen Sie besonders auf die korrekte Aussprache achten. Eine Liste mit Aussprachehilfen zu den schwierigeren der im Lehrwerk vorkommenden **Eigennamen** befindet sich auf Seite 148.

Unit 0

1	**what's** [wɒts]	= **what is** [wɒt ɪz]	was ist
	name [neɪm]	name: Elizabeth Taylor	Name
	his [hɪz]	~ name: Tony	sein(e)
	her [hɜː]	~ name: Elizabeth	ihr(e)
	What's his name?		Wie heißt er?
	His name is . . .		Er heißt . . .
	I'm [aɪm]	= **I am** [aɪ æm]	ich bin
	Hello [həˈləʊ]	H~, Elizabeth. - H~, Tony.	Hallo, guten Tag.
	my [maɪ]	I'm Tony. = M~ name is Tony.	mein(e)
	My name is . . .		Ich heiße . . .
	nice [naɪs]		nett, schön, angenehm
	to [tʊ]		*hier:* zu
	to meet [miːt]	Nice to ~ you.	(jemanden) treffen, kennenlernen
	you [juː]	I - ~	du, Sie; dich
	Nice to meet you.		*Begrüßungsfloskel, etwa:* Sehr erfreut.
	too [tuː]	Elizabeth is nice. Tony is nice, ~.	auch

are [ɑː]	I am Tarzan, you ~ Jane.	bist, sind
how [haʊ]		wie
How are you?		Wie geht's? Wie geht es Ihnen?
fine [faɪn]	≈ nice	fein, gut
thanks [θæŋks]	How are you? – I'm fine, ~.	danke
Fine, thanks.		Danke, gut.
and [ænd, ənd]	you ~ I; Tony ~ Elizabeth	und
thank you ['θæŋk jʊ]	= thanks	danke (schön)
I'm fine, thank you.		Danke, mir geht's gut.
this [ðɪs]	What's ~?	diese(r, s); dies, das
wife [waɪf]	I'm Peter White. Helen White is my ~.	(Ehe-)Frau
How do you do?	How do you do? – How do you do?	*(förmliche) Vorstellungsformel; etwa:* Guten Tag.
your [jɔː]	**[!]** I – my, you – ~	dein(e), Ihr(e)
Helen's ['helɪnz]	Helen's name is White.	Helens
pen [pen]		Füller, Kugelschreiber
pencil ['pensl]		Bleistift
hand-bag ['hændbæg]		Handtasche
book [bʊk]		Buch
lighter ['laɪtə]		Feuerzeug
yes [jes]	Are you Tony? – Y~, I am.	ja
it [ɪt]	Is this your pen? – Yes, ~ is.	es
no [nəʊ]	*opposite:* yes	nein
not [nɒt]		nicht
isn't [ɪznt]	= is **not** [nɒt]	ist nicht
it's [ɪts]	= it is [ɪt 'ɪz]	es ist
It's Peter's.	Is this your book? – No, it isn't, ~.	Es (er, sie) gehört Peter.
why [waɪ]	W~ is your name Muhammad Ali?	warum
that [ðæt]	Is ~ Helen's coat? – No, it isn't.	jene(r, s); der, die, das (da)
coat [kəʊt]		Mantel

Unit 1

whose [huːz]	W~ coat is it? – Peter's.	wessen
Whose . . . is this?		Wem gehört diese(r, s) . . . ?
who [huː]	W~ are you? What's your name?	wer
lady ['leɪdɪ]		Dame
over there ['əʊvə 'ðeə]	Not here, ~.	dort, da drüben
that's not a		das ist keine
where [weə]	That's not my coat. W~'s my coat?	wo
from [frɒm]	I'm ~ Berlin. I'm a Berliner.	von, aus
Where are you from?		Woher kommst du/ kommen Sie?
a [ə]	*vor Vokalen:* **an** [ən]	ein(e)
city ['sɪtɪ]	Berlin is a ~, and London is a ~, too.	(Groß-)Stadt
in [ɪn]	Where's my lighter? – It's ~ your hand-bag.	in
town [taʊn]	Rothenburg is a ~, and Swansea is a ~, too.	Stadt
village ['vɪlɪdʒ]	Klausdorf is a ~, and West Wickham is a ~, too.	Dorf
near [nɪə]	West Wickham is ~ London.	nahe, in der Nähe (von)

A 5	**can** [kæn/kən]	What ~ I do?	können, kann(st), könnt
	to spell [spel]	Can you ~ your name? – Yes: T-o-n-y.	buchstabieren
	please [pli:z]	Can you spell that, ~?	bitte
	Mr (Mister) [ˈmɪstə]	Are you Mr Miller? – No, I'm Peter White.	Herr *(vor Namen)*
	Mrs [ˈmɪsɪz]	Are you Mrs White? – Yes, I'm Helen White.	Frau *(vor Namen)*
	Miss [mɪs]	Are you Miss Miller? – Yes, I'm Nancy Miller.	Fräulein *(meist vor Namen)*
	good [gʊd]	≈ nice, fine	gut
	evening [ˈi:vnɪŋ]	It's a nice ~. – Yes, it is.	Abend
	Good evening.	Hello, Nancy. – ~, Mrs Miller.	Guten Abend.
	first [fɜ:st]	Unit 1 = ~ Unit	erst(e)
	first name	I'm Tony Miller. My ~ is Tony.	Vorname
	here [hɪə]	Where's my lighter? – It's ~, in my hand-bag.	hier
	key [ki:]		Schlüssel
A 6	**he** [hi:]	I – you – ~	er
	on [ɒn]	Where's my pen? – On that book over there.	auf
	business [ˈbɪznɪs]	Muhammad Ali: Boxing is my ~.	Geschäft
	on business	Is your wife here, too? – No, I'm here ~.	geschäftlich
	sales **manager** [ˈseɪlz ˈmænɪdʒə]		Verkaufsleiter
	actor [ˈæktə]	Marlon Brando is an ~.	Schauspieler
	new [nju:]	EfE is my ~ English book.	neu
	housewife [ˈhaʊswaɪf]	I'm Peter's wife. I'm a ~.	Hausfrau
	she [ʃi:]	I – you – he – ~	sie
	job [dʒɒb]	What's your ~? – I'm an actor.	Arbeit, Beruf
	What's his job?		Was ist er (von Beruf)?
	businessman [ˈbɪznɪsmæn]	I'm here on business. I'm a ~.	Geschäftsmann
	car [kɑ:]	This is my ~. It's a Ford.	Auto, Wagen
	in front of [ɪn ˈfrʌnt əv]	Where's your car? – It's ~ the hotel.	vor *(örtlich)*
	the [ðə], *vor Vokalen* [ðɪ]	the car, the actor	der, die, das
	hotel [həʊˈtel]	**[!]**; = *German*	*Hotel*
A 7	**to listen** [ˈlɪsn]		(zu)hören
B	**but** [bʌt]	Tony is not here, ~ his wife is.	aber
	to think [θɪŋk]	It's his car, I ~.	denken, glauben, meinen
	again [əˈgen]	K-E-Y. – Oh, can you spell that ~, please?	wieder, noch einmal
	Nice to meet you again.		Nett, Sie wiederzusehen.
	Well, . . . [wel]		*(Ausdruck, mit dem man eine Äußerung einleitet, etwa:)* Nun ja . . . . Also, . . .
	very [ˈverɪ]	A Rolls-Royce is a ~ good car.	sehr
	well [wel]	I'm very ~, thank you.	gut
	with [wɪð]	I'm here ~ my wife.	mit; bei
	I'm afraid [əˈfreɪd]	I ~ she's not here.	ich fürchte
	No, she isn't, I'm afraid.		Nein, leider nicht.
	for [fɔ:]	This key is ~ you.	für
	boat show [ˈbəʊt ʃəʊ]	Is the ~ in Hamburg or in Düsseldorf?	Bootsausstellung
	I'm here for the boat show.		Ich bin wegen der Bootsausstellung hier.
	husband [ˈhʌzbənd]	She's my wife. I'm her ~.	(Ehe-)Mann
	cigarette [sɪgəˈret]	**[!]**; = *German*	Zigarette
	dear [dɪə]	*Peter:* Helen! – *Helen:* Yes, ~?	Liebling
	Here you are.	My coat, please. – ~.	Bitte schön (hier ist, was sie wünschen).
	a lot [ə ˈlɒt]	40 cigarettes in an evening? That's ~!	viel(e)
	Thanks a lot.		Danke vielmals.

man [mæn], *pl.* men [men]	Who is that ~ in your car? – That's my husband.	Mann, Herr
at [æt]		an, auf, zu
at the **bar** [bɑː]	Where is he? – A~.	an der Bar
reception [rɪ'sepʃn]		Empfang
only ['əʊnlɪ]	What's your job? – I'm "~" a housewife.	nur
right [raɪt]	Yes, that's ~.	richtig
You're right.		Du hast/Sie haben recht.
to be [biː]	I am, you are, he/she/it is. To be or not to be that is the question. (Hamlet)	sein
to write [raɪt]	You ~ with a pen, a pencil, etc.	schreiben
to say [seɪ]	Please listen to what I ~.	sagen
question ['kwestʃən]	"What's your name?" is a ~.	Frage
short answer [ʃɔːt 'ɑːnsə]		kurze Antwort, Kurzantwort
to answer ['ɑːnsə]	Can you ~ this: "Where is Muhammad Ali from?"	(be)antworten
or [ɔː]	Are you from Berlin ~ from Hamburg?	oder
to ask [ɑːsk]	*opposite:* to answer	fragen

Unit 2

number ['nʌmbə] (= No.)	The ~ of this unit is 2.	Zahl, Nummer, Ziffer
house [haʊs], *pl.* houses ['haʊzɪz]		Haus
the number of your house		die Nummer Ihres Hauses, Ihre Hausnummer
What is there in . . . ?		Was ist in . . . ?, Was gibt es in . . . ?
living-room ['lɪvɪŋrʊm]	Mr and Mrs Scott are in the ~.	Wohnzimmer
there is ['ðeər'ɪz]	= there's [ðeəz]	da ist, es gibt
there are ['ðeər'ɑː, 'ðərə]	(→ 1/A3 over there)	da sind, es gibt
desk [desk]	The book is on your ~.	(Schreib-)Tisch
armchair [ɑːm'tʃeə]	There are two ~s in my living-room.	Sessel
lamp [læmp]	There's a new ~ on my desk.	Lampe
table ['teɪbl]	The cigarettes are on the ~.	Tisch
TV [tiː'viː]	= **television** ['telɪvɪʒn]	Fernsehen; Fernseher
chair [tʃeə]	There are four ~s and a table.	Stuhl
picture ['pɪktʃə]	The ~s in this book are nice.	Bild
shelf [ʃelf], *pl.* shelves [ʃelvz]	The books on the ~ are Peter's.	Wandbrett, Regal
a lot of [ə 'lɒt əv]	(→ 1/B a lot, A2 how many?)	viel(e), eine Menge
There are . . . books on the shelf.		Im Regal stehen . . . Bücher.
how many ['menɪ]	H~ cars are there? – Two.	wieviel(e)
none [nʌn]	How many are there? ~	kein(e,s,er)
comfortable ['kʌmfətəbl]	[!] This armchair is very ~.	bequem
quite [kwaɪt]	It's not very nice. – Oh, it's ~ nice.	ganz, ziemlich
old [əʊld]	He's 85. He's a very ~ man.	alt
expensive [ɪk'spensɪv]	£200 for a coat is very ~.	teuer
how much [mʌtʃ]		wieviel
How much is it?		Was kostet es?
on the **left** [left]		auf der linken Seite, links

	on the **right** [raɪt]		auf der rechten Seite, rechts
	in the **middle** ['mɪdl]		in der Mitte
	pound (£) [paʊnd]	This book is two ~s. (£2)	Pfund *(englische Währung)*
	p [pi:]; **penny,** *pl.* **pence** ['penɪ, pens]	£1 = 100 p	Penny *(englische Währung)*
A 5	**bedroom** ['bedrʊm]	There are two ~s in this flat.	Schlafzimmer
	kitchen ['kɪtʃɪn]	My husband is in the ~.	Küche
	bath, bathroom [bɑ:θ, 'bɑ:θrʊm]	The ~ is near the bedroom.	Bad(ezimmer)
	toilet ['tɔɪlɪt]	Where's the ~? – First on the left.	Toilette, WC
	flat [flæt]	There are 3 ~s in this house.	Wohnung
	modern ['mɒdən]	**[!]** not old	modern
	block (of flats) [blɒk]	There are 80 flats in this ~.	Wohnblock
	WC [dʌblju:'si:]	toilet	Toilette, WC
	garage ['gærɑ:ʒ]	**[!]** The car is in the ~.	Garage
	garden ['gɑ:dn]	The ~ is in front of the house.	Garten
	tree [tri:]	There are two ~s in the garden.	Baum
	week [wi:k]		Woche
	per week [pə]	= (for) a week	pro Woche
	basement ['beɪsmənt]		Keller
	basement flat	a flat in the basement	Souterrainwohnung
	room [ru:m]	How's your hotel ~? – Very nice.	Zimmer
	central ['sentrəl]	in the middle of	zentral, im Zentrum von
	quiet ['kwaɪət]	**[!]** It's a very ~ village. There are no cars.	ruhig
	street [stri:t]	There are a lot of cars in this ~.	Straße
	from . . . to . . .	(→ 1/A4 from)	von . . . bis . . .
A 6	**me** [mi:]	I – my – ~	mir, mich
	to tell [tel]	T~ me your name. = Say what your name is.	erzählen, sagen
	about [ə'baʊt]	Tell me ~ your job.	über, von
	to live [lɪv]	I ~ in a house, not a flat.	leben; wohnen
	minute ['mɪnɪt]	**[!]**; = *German*	Minute
	hour ['aʊə]	60 minutes = 1 ~	Stunde
	half [hɑ:f]	1/2, 0.5	Hälfte; halb
	half an hour		eine halbe Stunde
	by car [baɪ]		mit dem Auto
	bus [bʌs]	**[!]**; = *German*	(Auto-)Bus, Linienbus
	Underground ['ʌndəgraʊnd]	The "Metro" is the name of the ~ in Paris.	U-Bahn
	on foot [fʊt]	not by car or bus	zu Fuß
	park [pɑ:k]	= *German*	Park
	flower ['flaʊə]	There are a lot of ~s in the garden.	Blume
	to see [si:]	Can you ~ my car? It's in front of the house.	sehen
	you can see		*hier:* man kann sehen
	window ['wɪndəʊ]	I can see the garden from my ~.	Fenster
	class [klɑ:s]		Klasse
	to get out of		*hier:* sich hinausscheren
A 7	**really** ['rɪəlɪ]	R~? Is that right?	wirklich, tatsächlich
	not really		eigentlich nicht
	cheap [tʃi:p]	not expensive	billig
	What about . . . ?		Wie ist es/das mit . . . ?
	sometimes ['sʌmtaɪmz]	I ~ meet Betty on the bus.	manchmal
	difficult ['dɪfɪklt]	English isn't ~.	schwierig
	to find [faɪnd]	F~ the answer to this question.	finden, suchen
B	**How's . . . ?**	= How is . . . ?	Wie ist . . . ?, *hier:* Was macht . . . ?

zoo [zu:]	**[!]**; = *German*	Zoo
to hear [hɪə]	Quiet! I can ~ his car. (≠ 1/A7 to listen)	hören
animal ['ænɪml]	There are a lot of ~s in the zoo.	Tier
to know [nəʊ]	I ~ the answer to this question.	wissen, kennen
you know		wissen Sie, weißt du
colour TV ['kʌlə]		Farbfernsehen, Farbfernseher
£6 **a week**	£6 per week (→ A5)	die Woche, pro Woche
entrance ['entrəns]	Where's the ~ to the zoo?	Eingang
traffic ['træfɪk]	a lot of cars and buses in a street = a lot of ~	Verkehr
even ['i:vn]	It isn't difficult, ~ I can do it.	sogar
night [naɪt]		Nacht
at night		nachts
student ['stju:dnt]	**[!]**; = *German*	Student, Kursteilnehmer
right [raɪt]	1 + 1 = 2. That's ~. (→ 1/B)	richtig
wrong [rɒŋ]	*opposite:* right	falsch

3

Unit 3

airport ['eəpɔ:t]	Heathrow is a London ~.	Flughafen
at the airport	(→ 1/B at the bar)	am/auf dem Flughafen
they [ðeɪ]	he + she = ~	sie *(pl.)*
these [ði:z]	this book, ~ books	diese, die (hier)
their [ðeə]	his book + her book = ~ books	ihr(e)
child [tʃaɪld], *pl.* children ['tʃɪldrən]	**[!]**	Kind
family ['fæməlɪ]	~ = wife + husband + child(ren)	Familie
family name	My first name is Jack, my ~ is Miller.	Nachname
to win [wɪn]	You can ~ a car, a boat or books.	gewinnen
weekend [wi:k'end]	**[!]** (→ 2/A5 week)	Wochenende
trip [trɪp]	a ~ to London	Ausflug, Reise
weekend trip ['wi:kend 'trɪp]		Wochenendreise
ideal [aɪ'dɪəl]	**[!]** He's the ~ husband.	ideal
to like [laɪk]	I ~ the Beatles.	mögen, gernhaben
British ['brɪtɪʃ]	English – British	britisch
address [ə'dres]	**[!]** where you live	Adresse, Anschrift
we [wi:]	you + I = ~	wir
our [aʊə]	your book + my book = ~ books	unser(e)
time [taɪm]	minutes + hours + weeks	Zeit
What's the time, please?	(→ 0/1 What's his name?)	Wieviel Uhr ist es, bitte?
morning ['mɔ:nɪŋ]	3.00-12.00	Morgen, Vormittag
afternoon [ɑ:ftə'nu:n]	12.00-18.00	Nachmittag
evening ['i:vnɪŋ]	18.00-24.00 (→ 1/A5 Good ~.)	Abend
a.m. [eɪ'em]	= in the morning	morgens, vormittags
p.m. [pi:'em]	= in the afternoon/evening	nachmittags, abends
clock [klɒk]	What's the time, please? – Look, there's a ~ over there.	(Wand-, Turm-, Stand-)Uhr
five **o'clock** [ə'klɒk]	5.00	fünf Uhr
when [wen]		wann
next [nekst]	Not this week, but ~ week.	nächst(e)
at [æt]	The next bus is ~ five o'clock.	um
one [wʌn]	There's ~ at six o'clock.	eine(r, s)
What time is it?	= What's the time?	Wie spät ist es?
five **to** three [tʊ]	3 o'clock – 5 minutes	fünf vor drei
five **past** three [pɑ:st]	3 o'clock + 5 minutes	fünf nach drei

	a **quarter** past three [ˈkwɔːtə]	3 o'clock + 15 minutes	Viertel nach drei, viertel vier
	half past three [hɑːf]	3 o'clock + 30 minutes (→ 2/A6 half)	halb vier (!)
	must [mʌst]	M~ you go?	müssen, muß(t), müßt
	to leave [liːv]	Yes, I'm afraid I must ~.	losgehen, aufbrechen, abfahren
	English class	(→ 2/A6 class)	Englischunterricht, -stunde
	what time is	= when is	um welche Zeit/wann geht
	after [ˈɑːftə]	The streets are quiet ~ 10 p.m.	nach *(zeitlich)*
A5	**train** [treɪn]	The new IC ~s are very comfortable.	Zug
	at nine **oh** four [əʊ]	9.04	um 9.04 Uhr
A7	**flight** [flaɪt]	Lufthansa ~ LH 037 from London to Frankfurt is at 8.40.	Flug
	to go [gəʊ]	You can ~ by car or by bus.	gehen, fahren
	where [weə]	W~ can we go? – To the bar.	wohin
	gate [geɪt]		*hier:* Flugsteig, Ausgang
A8	**to excuse** [ɪkˈskjuːz]		entschuldigen
	Excuse me, . . .	~, what's the time, please?	*jemanden ansprechen:* Entschuldigen Sie bitte, . . .
	to get [get]	You can ~ a whisky at the bar.	bekommen
	jeans [dʒiːnz]	= *German*	Jeans
	shirt [ʃɜːt]		Hemd
	T-**shirt** [ˈtiːʃɜːt]	= *German*	T-Shirt
	shoe [ʃuː]	Where can I get ~s?	Schuh
	blouse [blaʊz]	**[!]** man: shirt, lady: ~	Bluse
	skirt [skɜːt]	I must get a new ~ and a blouse.	Rock
	radio [ˈreɪdɪəʊ]	**[!]**, – *German*	Radio
	record [ˈrekɔːd]	**[!]** Is this a new Beatles ~?	Schallplatte
	suitcase [ˈsuːtkeɪs]	**[!]** After a flight it is sometimes difficult to find your ~.	Koffer
	postcard [ˈpəʊstkɑːd]		Postkarte
	picture postcard	a postcard with a picture on it	Ansichtskarte
	floor [flɔː]	There are a lot of ~s in a modern block of flats.	Stock(werk), Etage
	first [fɜːst] 1st	Unit 1 = the ~ Unit (→ 1/A5 first name)	erste(r, s)
	second [ˈsekənd] 2nd	Unit 2 = the ~ Unit	zweite(r, s)
	third [θɜːd] 3rd	Unit 3 = the ~ Unit	dritte(r, s)
	fourth [fɔːθ] 4th	Unit 4 = the ~ Unit	vierte(r, s)
	ground floor [graʊnd]	the first floor over the basement	Erdgeschoß
	Thank you very much.	= Thanks a lot. (→ 1/B)	Danke vielmals. Vielen Dank.
A9	**stamp** [stæmp]	Where can I get ~s?	Briefmarke
	post office [ˈpəʊst ɒfɪs]	You can get stamps at the ~.	Postamt
	shop [ʃɒp]	Where can I get shoes? – At the shoe ~ in George Street.	Laden, Geschäft
	bank [bæŋk]	Where can I get English pounds? – At a ~.	Bank
	book shop	Where can I get books? – At ~s.	Buchhandlung
	a chemist's [ˈkemɪsts]	**[!]**	eine Apotheke
	along [əˈlɒŋ]	Go ~ this street here.	entlang
	next to [ˈnekstə]	The bank is over there, ~ the post office.	neben
	Not at all. [ɔːl]	Thank you. – ~. (≠ Here you are. → 1/B)	Bitte sehr. *(als Antwort auf eine Entschuldigung, auf Dank)*
	to buy [baɪ]	I can't ~ this coat, it's very expensive.	kaufen

information [ɪnfəˈmeɪʃn]	**[!]**; = *German*	Information, Auskunft
information desk	Ask at the ~ when the flight to London is.	Information(sstand)
department store [dɪˈpɑ:tmənt stɔ:]		Kaufhaus, Warenhaus
men [men]	**[!]** *pl. of* man (→ 1/B)	Männer, Herren
clothes [kləʊðz]	**[!]** Skirts, blouses, jeans, etc. are ~.	Kleidung
those [ðəʊz]	this – these, that – ~	jene, die (da)
I'd like [aɪd] = **I would like** [wʊd]	I like T-shirts. ~ a T-shirt with my name on it. (→ A2 to like)	ich möchte (gern), ich will
this one	What about ~? (→ A3)	dies(e, er, es) hier
shopping **trip** [ˈʃɒpɪŋ trɪp]	I'd like to buy a lot of clothes. What about a ~ to London? (→ A2 trip; A9 shop)	Einkaufsfahrt
friend [frend]	Nancy is not my wife, she's a ~.	Freund(in), Bekannte(r)
open [ˈəʊpən]	The shops are ~ from 9 to 6.	offen, geöffnet
this afternoon	from 12 to 6 p.m.	heute nachmittag
on Saturday [ˈsætədɪ]		samstags, sonnabends, am Samstag
alright [ɔ:lˈraɪt]	You can also spell it "all right".	in Ordnung
Monday [ˈmʌndɪ]	Saturday → Sunday → ~	Montag
from [frɒm]	We can get the records ~ HMV. (→ 1/A4 from)	von
first [fɜ:st]	F~ I ask for a new record, (→ A8)	zuerst
then [ðen]	~ I listen to it in the shop,	dann
after that	and ~ I buy it. (→ A4 after)	danach
to go sight-seeing [ˈsaɪtsi:ɪŋ]	to go and see a town, city, old houses, etc.	Sehenswürdigkeiten besichtigen
Sunday [ˈsʌndɪ]	the weekend = Saturday and ~	Sonntag
closed [kləʊzd]	**[!]** not open	geschlossen
parcel [ˈpɑ:sl]	Open this ~, please. I'd like to see what's in it.	Päckchen, Paket
Pardon? [ˈpɑ:dn]	Can you say that again, please?	Wie bitte? Verzeihung?
bag [bæg]	You get (plastic) ~s at shops and department stores. (→ 0/3 hand-bag)	(Plastik-)Tüte, Tasche, Beutel
can't [kɑ:nt]	= cannot	kann(st)/können nicht
to do [du:]	What can we ~ on Sunday? – Not very much. (0/2 How do you do?)	tun
in there		da drin
now [naʊ]	What's the time ~? – 8 o'clock.	nun, jetzt
lost property office [lɒst ˈprɒpətɪ ɒfɪs]	I can't find my keys. – Go to the ~. (→ A9 post office)	Fundbüro
you [ju:] *pl.*	we – ~ – they	ihr, Sie
girlfriend [ˈgɜ:lfrend]	Mary is John's ~. (→ B friend)	Freundin
your [jɔ:] *pl.*	**[!]** our books – ~ books – their books	euer(e), Ihr(e)
to go shopping	to go to shops and department stores and buy clothes, records, etc. (→ B shopping trip)	einkaufen (gehen)
of course [əv ˈkɔ:s]	Can you read this? – O~ I can.	natürlich, klar

Unit 4

to borrow [ˈbɒrəʊ]	I can't find my pen. Can I ~ your pencil?	borgen
have (got) [hæv gɒt]	I haven't got a pencil.	haben, besitzen
(I'm) sorry [ˈsɒrɪ]		es tut mir leid
No, I'm sorry, I haven't.	(→ 1/B I'm afraid)	Nein, leider nicht.
moment [ˈməʊmənt]	**[!]**; = *German;* for a ~ ≈ for a minute	Moment, Augenblick

A 2	Yes, I have.		Ja.
	No, I haven't.		Nein.
	year [jɪə]	52 weeks = 1 ~	Jahr
A 5	**to help** [help]	Can I ~ you?	helfen
	us [ʌs]	I - me, we - ~	uns
	matter ['mætə]		Sache
	What's the matter?	≈ What's wrong?	Was ist los?
	something ['sʌmθɪŋ]	Quiet! I can hear ~. What is it?	etwas
	There's something wrong with it.		Etwas stimmt damit nicht.
	to let [let]	We must do it, so ~ us do it now.	lassen
	Let's go.	= Let us go.	Gehen wir.
	Well, let's see.		Nun, wir wollen mal sehen.
	But Jim can.		Aber Jim kann es.
	you [ju:] *pl.*	I - me, you - you (→ 3/C1 you *pl.*)	euch, Ihnen
	him [hɪm]	he - ~	ihn, ihm
	her [hɜ:]	she - ~	sie, ihr
	them [ðem]	they - ~	sie, ihnen
A 6	**kind** [kaɪnd]	We can have Peter's car for the weekend. - That's very ~ of him.	freundlich, nett
A 7	**son** [sʌn]	The Queen has 4 children. Charles is her ~.	Sohn
	daughter ['dɔ:tə]	Anne is her ~.	Tochter
	brother ['brʌðə]	Charles is Anne's ~.	Bruder
	sister ['sɪstə]	Anne is Charles' ~.	Schwester
	father ['fɑ:ðə]	Prince Philip is their ~.	Vater
	mother ['mʌðə]	The Queen is their ~.	Mutter
	grandfather ['grændfɑ:ðə]	your father's or mother's father	Großvater
	mother-in-law ['mʌðərɪnlɔ:]	your wife's or husband's mother	Schwiegermutter
	parents ['peərənts]	Your father and mother are your ~.	Eltern
	uncle ['ʌŋkl]	your father's or mother's brother	Onkel
	aunt [ɑ:nt]	your father's or mother's sister	Tante
A 8	**day** [deɪ]	24 hours = 1 ~	Tag
	today [tə'deɪ]	this day	heute
	What day is it today?	(→ 3/A4 What time is it?)	Was für ein Tag ist heute?
	birthday ['bɜ:θdeɪ]	I'm 40 today. Today is my ~.	Geburtstag
	on 2nd May	on the second of May	am 2. Mai
A 9	**present** ['preznt]	[!] You get a lot of ~s on your birthday.	Geschenk
	back [bæk]	My husband is ~ from his weekend trip to London.	zurück
	piece [pi:s]		Stück
	chewing-gum ['tʃu:ɪŋgʌm]		Kaugummi
	a piece of chewing-gum		ein Stück Kaugummi
	chocolate ['tʃɒklət]	[!] Children like chewing-gum and ~.	Schokolade
	bar [bɑ:]	This ~ of chocolate is 50p.	Tafel
	puzzle ['pʌzl]	This ~ is very difficult. It has a lot of pieces.	Rätsel, *hier:* Zusammensetzspiel
	thing [θɪŋ]	Can we leave our ~s in the car?	Ding, Sache
	ticket ['tɪkɪt]	When you go by Underground, you must buy a ~ first.	(Eintritts-, Fahr-)Karte
	concert ['kɒnsət]	[!]; = *German*	Konzert
	Christmas ['krɪsməs]	25th December is ~ Day.	Weihnachten
	this is what		hier/das ist, was
	umbrella [ʌm'brelə]	In London you can see a lot of men with ~s.	(Regen-)Schirm

0	**nothing** [ˈnʌθɪŋ]	What have you got in your hand? – N~. (→ something 4/A5)	nichts
	not yet [jet]	I'm ~ 21, I'm only 20.	noch nicht
	no [nəʊ]	N~ chocolate for me, thank you.	kein(e)
	idea [aɪˈdɪə]	**[!]** Let's buy the Christmas presents now. – That's a good ~.	Idee
1	**What a** nice lighter!		Was für ein schönes Feuerzeug!
2	**film** [fɪlm]	= *German*	Film
	on TV	You can see a lot of old films ~.	im Fernsehen
	cinema [ˈsɪnəmə]	where you go and see films	Kino
	Is there a good film on at the cinema?		Läuft im Kino ein guter Film?
	tonight [təˈnaɪt]	this evening (→ A8 today)	heute abend/nacht
	tomorrow [təˈmɒrəʊ]	Today is Saturday, ~ is Sunday.	morgen
	tomorrow night		morgen abend
	Yes, there is.		Ja.
	No, there isn't.		Nein.
	bad [bæd]	*opposite:* good	schlecht
3	**good night**	(→ 1/A5 good evening)	gute Nacht
	Oh dear! [dɪə]		Ach du meine Güte!
	when [wen]	When are you leaving? – W~ he's back.	wenn
	more [mɔː]	I haven't got time now. We can do it when I've got ~ time.	mehr
	Mummy [ˈmʌmɪ]		Mama, Mutti
	We're going to the cinema tonight.		Heute abend gehen wir ins Kino.
	to rain [reɪn]	You must have an umbrella when it is raining.	regnen
	It's raining.		Es regnet.
	Dad [dæd]		Papa, Vati
	to play [pleɪ]	A lot of children ~ in the street even when there is a lot of traffic.	spielen
	Memory [ˈmeməri]		Memory *(Gedächtnis-spiel)*
	baby-sitter [ˈbeɪbɪsɪtə]	**[!]**; = *German*	Babysitter
	to come [kʌm]	*opposite:* to go	kommen
	is coming [ˈkʌmɪŋ]		kommt
	enough [ɪˈnʌf]	I live in a flat. I haven't got ~ money for a house.	genug
	money [ˈmʌnɪ]	Pounds and pence are English ~.	Geld
	We're going by car.		Wir fahren mit dem Auto.
	then [ðen]	He isn't here. – Where is he ~?	denn, dann
	that [ðæt, ðət]	I know ~ he can't come.	. . . , daß
	tooth, [tuːθ], *pl.* teeth [tiːθ]	We have 32 teeth.	Zahn, Zähne
	to take [teɪk]	Can I ~ your coat, sir?	nehmen
	letter [ˈletə]	Buy a stamp at the post office for this ~.	Brief
	night-night [ˈnaɪtˈnaɪt]	good night	gute Nacht *(Kinder-sprache)*
	bye-bye [baɪˈbaɪ]		auf Wiedersehn, tschüs
	drink [drɪŋk]	Coca-cola and whisky are ~s.	Getränk
	a drink for you		etwas zu trinken für Sie
	come on	C~, we must leave now.	komm doch, beeil dich
	late [leɪt]	It's 11 p.m. It's ~. We must go now.	spät
6	**month** [mʌnθ]	A year = 12 ~s.	Monat
1	**to read** [riːd]	You can ~ books and letters.	lesen

D2	**to fill in** [fɪl]	F~ "from" or "to": I'm . . . London.	einsetzen
	we can let him have	(→ A5 to let)	wir können ihm geben
	madam [ˈmædəm]	*Lady:* Can you help me, please? – Yes, ~.	gnädige Frau *(Anrede für eine Dame, benutzt von Kellnern, Verkäufern, Beamten etc.)*
D5	boyfriend [ˈbɔɪfrend]	John is Mary's ~. (→ 3/C1 girlfriend)	Freund
D6	*dep* = **departure** [dɪˈpɑːtʃə]	when the bus or train leaves	Abfahrt
	arr = **arrival** [əˈraɪvl]	when the bus or train comes	Ankunft
D7	the keys to the car		die Wagenschlüssel
	the tickets for the cinema		die Kinokarten

Unit 5

A1	**to speak (to)** [spiːk]	You ~ German and English. (≠ to say 1/C4; ≠ to tell 2/A6)	sprechen (mit)
	Yes, speaking.		Ja, am Apparat.
	other [ˈʌðə]	Here are two letters, one is for you, the ~ is for me.	andere(r, s)
	phone [fəʊn]	My ~ number is 82 63 45.	Telefon
	on the other phone		am anderen Apparat
	to ring [rɪŋ]	Can you ~ me this evening?	läuten, klingeln; anrufen
	Goodbye. [gʊdˈbaɪ]	= Bye-bye (→ 4/B).	Auf Wiedersehen.
A2	**at home** [həʊm]	You're ~ when you are in your house or flat.	zu Hause
	Is he in?	= Is he at home?	Ist er zu Hause?
	No, he's out. [aʊt]	– No, he isn't at home.	Nein, er ist ausgegangen.
A3	**line** [laɪn]	It's a bad ~, I can't hear you.	*hier:* Leitung, Verbindung
	S for Samuel. [ˈsæmjʊəl]	(→ 1/B for)	S wie Samuel.
A4	**to phone** [fəʊn]	= to ring	anrufen
	reception desk	(→ 1/B reception)	Empfang
	at the moment	now (→ 4/A1 moment)	im Moment
	just [dʒʌst]	= at this moment	(jetzt) gerade
	to drink [drɪŋk]	to have a drink (→ 4/B a drink)	trinken
	tea [tiː]	In England they drink a lot of ~.	Tee
	cup [kʌp]	You drink tea from it.	Tasse
	a cup of tea		eine Tasse Tee
	to leave for	to leave the house and go to (→ 3/A4 to leave)	gehen zu/ins/. . .
	to come along [əˈlɒŋ]	Are you coming along? = Are you coming with me? (→ 3/A9 along)	mitkommen
	to look [lʊk]	L~, can you see him?	sehen, (hin)schauen
	taxi [ˈtæksɪ]	**[!]**; = *German*	Taxi
A5	This is John speaking.		Hier spricht John.
	to sit [sɪt]	You can ~ on that chair.	sitzen
	to watch [wɒtʃ]	Let's ~ the show. I'd like to see it. (see ≠ ~; hear ≠ listen)	beobachten, anschauen
	to watch TV	Let's ~. What's on tonight?	fernsehen
	to go out	to leave the house	ausgehen

Western [ˈwestən]	= *German*	Wildwestfilm
cowboy [ˈkaʊbɔɪ]	= *German*	Cowboy, Viehtreiber
He is in it.	He plays in the film, show, etc.	Er spielt mit.
great [greɪt]	= very good	*hier:* großartig
over [ˈəʊvə]	(→ 1/A3 over there)	über, herüber
Come over then.		Komm(t) doch herüber.
to hurry [ˈhʌrɪ]	My train leaves in 10 minutes. I must ~.	(sich be)eilen
See you in a minute.	(→ 2/A6 to see, minute)	Bis gleich.
'Bye. [baɪ]	= Bye-bye (→ 4/B; A1)	Tschüs.
to look at	≈ to watch (→ A4 to look)	(sich) ansehen, betrachten
holiday [ˈhɒlədɪ]	I take a month's ~ in July.	Ferien, Urlaub
to talk (about) [ˈtɔːk əˈbaʊt]	≈ to speak (about) (→ A1)	sprechen, reden (über)
out of	I leave = I go ~ the house	aus
to look out of the window		aus dem Fenster sehen
isn't it?	It's a nice day, ~?	nicht wahr?
to lie [laɪ]	The letter is lying on the table.	liegen
sun [sʌn]	On my holidays I lie in the ~ for hours.	Sonne
ice-cream [aɪsˈkriːm]	**[!]**	(Speise-)Eis
stand [stænd]	**[!]**; = *German*	Stand
to eat [iːt]	You drink tea, you ~ chocolate.	essen
Englishman [ˈɪŋglɪʃmən]	a man from England	Engländer
to open [ˈəʊpən]	You can ~ a window, your book, etc. (→ 3/B open)	öffnen, aufmachen
bottle [ˈbɒtl]	Can you open this ~ of whisky?	Flasche
wine [waɪn]	Beaujolais is a French ~.	Wein
red [red]	Chianti is a ~ Italian wine.	rot
white [waɪt]	Teeth are ~.	weiß
into [ˈɪntʊ]	*opposite:* out of	hinein
to stand [stænd]	to lie → to sit → to ~	stehen
famous [ˈfeɪməs]	Marlon Brando is a ~ actor.	berühmt
tower [ˈtaʊə]	The Toronto TV ~ is very famous.	Turm
was [wɒz]	I ~ a child, I'm a man/woman now.	war
to take a picture	(→ 2/A2 picture, 4/B to take)	ein Foto machen
dinner [ˈdɪnə]	We have ~ at 8 p.m.	Abendessen *(Hauptmahlzeit)*
glass [glɑːs]	a cup of tea, a ~ of wine	Glas
whisky [ˈwɪskɪ]		Whisky
to listen to [ˈlɪsn]	Let's ~ the radio. (→ 1/A7 to listen; A5 to watch)	zuhören
to work [wɜːk]	I ~ from 9 to 5. I ~ in a shop.	arbeiten
secretary [ˈsekrətrɪ]		Sekretär(in)
The bus **is late.**	(→ 4/B late)	Der Bus hat Verspätung.
to get on (the bus)		(in den Bus) einsteigen
No. [ˈnʌmbə]	(→ 2/A1 number)	Nummer
at her desk	(→ 1/B at the bar)	an ihrem Schreibtisch
office [ˈɒfɪs]	(→ 3/B lost property office)	Büro
policeman [pəˈliːsmən]	**[!]** He watches the traffic.	Polizist
to climb [klaɪm]	Can you ~ that tree?	klettern (auf)
through [θruː]	You can see ~ a window.	durch
burglar [ˈbɜːglə]	He takes your money, expensive things, etc. when you are not at home.	Einbrecher
officer [ˈɒfɪsə]	what you say to a policeman	Wachtmeister *(Anrede für einen Polizisten)*
neighbour [ˈneɪbə]	the person next to you	Nachbar(in)

	to turn on [tɜ:n]	T~ the radio. I'd like to listen to the concert.	einschalten
	light [laɪt]	*here:* lamp	Licht, Lampe
	to write down	(→ 1/C4 to write)	aufschreiben
	all (this) [ɔ:l]		(das) alles
	serious ['sɪərɪəs]	a ~ question	ernst
	door [dɔ:]	You go through it (into or out of a room).	Tür
	summer ['sʌmə]	~ = June to September	Sommer
C1	*progressive form* [prəʊ'gresɪv 'fɔ:m]		Verlaufsform
C2	**to go home**	*opposite:* to go out, to leave (→ A2 at home)	nach Hause gehen, fahren
D1	police officer		Polizeibeamter
D2	**story** ['stɔ:rɪ]	Can you tell me a good-night ~, Dad?	Geschichte
D3	*to shop* [ʃɒp]	= to go shopping (→ 3/A9 shop)	einkaufen
	tennis ['tenɪs]	= *German*	Tennis
	lunch [lʌntʃ]	We have ~ at 12.30. (→ A7 dinner)	(warmes) Mittagessen
	restaurant ['restərɒŋ]	[!]; = *German*	Restaurant
	to have a bath [bɑ:θ]	[!] (→ 2/A5 bath, bathroom)	ein Bad nehmen, baden
	school [sku:l]	[!] English children go to ~ when they are 5.	Schule
	bed [bed]	There are two ~s in Mr and Mrs Scott's bedroom. (→ 2/A5)	Bett
	He's in bed.		Er liegt im Bett.

Unit 6

A1	**people** ['pi:pl]	men – women – children = ~	Leute, Menschen
	often ['ɒfn]	*opposite:* sometimes (→ 2/A7)	oft, häufig
	newspaper ['nju:speɪpə]	The Washington Post is a famous American ~.	Zeitung
	theatre ['θɪətə]	[!] What's on at the ~ tonight?	Theater
	to wash [wɒʃ]	In the morning you ~ in the bathroom.	(sich) waschen
	alone [ə'ləʊn]	Are you ~? – No, Fred is here.	alleine
	less [les]	more or ~	weniger
A2	What do you do?	(→ 3/B to do)	Was machen Sie?
	always ['ɔ:lweɪz]	I ~ have my holidays in summer.	immer
	usually ['ju:ʒʊəlɪ]	I ~ leave the office at 5, but today I'm leaving at 6.	(für) gewöhnlich, meistens
	never ['nevə]	*opposite:* always	nie(mals)
A3	night school	Children go to school in the morning, you go to ~ in the evening. (→ 5/D3 school)	Abendschule
A4	**every** ['evrɪ]	~ day = on Monday, Tuesday, Wednesday, etc.	jede(r, s)
	to get up	I ~ at 6 and leave the house at 7 every morning.	aufstehen
	to make [meɪk]	I ~ the beds every morning.	machen
	breakfast ['brekfəst]	I usually have a cup of tea and some toast for ~. (→ lunch 5/D3, dinner 5/A7)	Frühstück
	washing-up [wɒʃɪŋ'ʌp]	On Sunday Peter helps Martha with the ~.	Abwasch
	to do the washing-up	to wash the cups etc. after breakfast, lunch or dinner	abwaschen
	same [seɪm]	Father sits in the ~ armchair every evening.	selbe, gleiche

in a hurry ['hʌrɪ]	I'm ~ = I must hurry. (→ 5/A5)	in Eile
to start [stɑːt]	I work from 9 to 5. I ~ at 9.	anfangen, beginnen
work [wɜːk]	Housework is ~, too. (→ 5/A7 to work)	Arbeit
to type [taɪp]	This is a business letter; I can't write it with a pen, I must ~ it.	tippen
(tea-)break [breɪk]		(Tee-)Pause
to smoke [sməʊk]	A lot of people ~ cigarettes.	rauchen
Dear [dɪə]	You start a letter with it. (→ 1/B dear)	*Briefanrede:* Liebe(r, s)/ Sehr geehrte(r, s) . . .
like [laɪk]		wie
This is what my day is like.		Mein Tag sieht folgendermaßen aus.
early ['ɜːlɪ]	*opposite:* late (→ 4/B, 5/A8)	früh
factory ['fæktərɪ]	In this ~ they make cars.	Fabrik
walk [wɔːk]	On Sunday afternoon I often go for a ~ in the park.	Spaziergang
dog [dɒg]	Lassie is a famous TV ~.	Hund
to go for a walk with the dog		den Hund ausführen
(phone) **call** [kɔːl]	to make a ~ = to ring, to phone (→ 5/A1)	(Telefon-)Anruf
to sell [sel]	*opposite:* to buy	verkaufen
coffee ['kɒfɪ]	In Germany we usually drink ~ for breakfast, in England they often have tea.	Kaffee
canteen [kæn'tiːn]	In a factory or in an office you can usually have lunch in a ~.	Kantine
to get home	to come home, to get back (→ 5/A2 at home)	nach Hause kommen
to have a cup of tea		eine Tasse Tee trinken
housework ['haʊswɜːk]	to do the ~ = to work in the house	Hausarbeit
to go to bed	I usually ~ at 10.30. (→ 5/D3 in bed)	ins Bett gehen
that's all for now		das ist im Augenblick alles
to hope [həʊp]	I ~ it isn't raining. I haven't got an umbrella.	hoffen
soon [suːn]	It's late. We must go ~.	bald
best [best]	This restaurant is very, very good. It's the ~ restaurant in town.	beste(r, s)
wish [wɪʃ]	I hope to see you soon = It's my ~ to see you soon.	Wunsch
with best wishes		mit den besten Grüßen
Yours,		*Briefformel:* Dein(e), Ihr(e)
so [səʊ]	**[!]**; = *German*	so
And why do you think so?		Und warum nehmen Sie das an/meinen Sie das?
because [bɪ'kɒz]	Why are you in a hurry? – B~ I'm late.	weil
to drive [draɪv]	I can ~ a car, but I can't ~ a bus.	fahren
colleague ['kɒliːg]	**[!]** He or she and you work in the same office.	Kollege, Kollegin
she does her shopping	she goes shopping (→ 3/D2)	sie erledigt ihre Einkäufe
missing ['mɪsɪŋ]	I've got three pens, but I can't find one of them. One is ~.	fehlend
word [wɜːd]	"T-shirt" is an English ~, and it is a German ~, too.	Wort
driver ['draɪvə]	A bus ~ drives a bus.	Fahrer(in)
during ['djʊərɪŋ]	You can see the sun ~ the day.	während
to get to the office	(→ A6 to get home)	im Büro ankommen, eintreffen
before [bɪ'fɔː]	~ → during → after	vor(her)

A 10	**to travel** ['trævl]	to go (by car, bus, underground)	fahren, reisen
	way [weɪ]	Can you tell me the ~ to the post office, please?	Weg
B	**strike** [straɪk]	They're on ~ = they aren't working.	Streik
	news [nju:z]	The information you hear on radio or TV or read in the newspaper.	Nachricht(en), Neuigkeiten
	already [ɔ:l'redɪ]	*opposite:* not yet	schon
	traffic-jam ['træfɪkdʒæm]	When all the cars and buses stop and can't go on, there's a ~.	Verkehrsstau
	road [rəʊd]	the *streets* of London, but: the ~ from London to Dover	(Land-)Straße
	since [sɪns]		seit
	to picket ['pɪkɪt]	Why are they ~ing? – So their colleagues can't work.	Streikposten stehen/aufstellen
	perhaps [pə'hæps]	Let's ask the policeman. P~ he can help us.	vielleicht
	somewhere ['sʌmweə]	I can't find my umbrella, but it must be ~. (→ 4/A5 something = *(irgend)etwas)*	irgendwo(hin)
	to park [pɑ:k]	to leave the car in the street *(= German)*	parken
	everyone ['evrɪwʌn]	In a village you know ~, in a city perhaps not even your neighbour.	jede(r)
	it takes me	I~ an hour to get to the office. (→ 4/B to take)	ich brauche
	an hour and a half		anderthalb Stunden
	nothing really	(→ 2/A7 really, 4/A10 nothing)	eigentlich nichts
	to need [ni:d]	You ~ (≈ must have) a pen to write a letter.	brauchen
	meeting ['mi:tɪŋ]	A lot of people are coming to the ~. (→ 0/1 to meet)	Versammlung, Treffen
	is that it?		ist es das?
	strike-breaker ['straɪk'breɪkə]	He works when his colleagues are on strike.	Streikbrecher
	I can't be a strike-breaker, can I?	I can't . . . , can I? (→ 5/A6 It is . . . , isn't it?)	Ich kann doch kein Streikbrecher sein, nicht wahr?
	high [haɪ]	The Toronto TV tower is 553 m ~.	hoch
	wage(s) ['weɪdʒ(ɪz)]	the money you get every week for a job	Lohn
	higher wages	more money for your work	höhere Löhne
	to mean [mi:n]	"Wages" ~s "Lohn" in German.	bedeuten, heißen
	price [praɪs]	What's the ~ of this coat? = How much is it?	Preis
	to pay [peɪ]	I'm sorry I can't ~, I haven't got enough money.	(be)zahlen
	boss [bɒs]	He tells you what you must do at the factory, at the office, etc.	Chef
	without [wɪ'ðaʊt]	You can't pay ~ money.	ohne
	we aren't speaking	(→ 5/A1 to speak)	wir sprechen nicht (mehr) miteinander
	because of [bɪ'kɒz əv]	I'm late ~ *the traffic-jam* = because there *was* a traffic-jam.	wegen des *Staus (aber:* weil ein Stau *war)*
	to understand [ʌndə'stænd]	I ~ = I know what it means.	verstehen, begreifen
	problem ['prɒbləm]	**[!]**; = *German*	Problem
	just like [dʒʌst]	(→ A6 like)	genau wie
	to walk [wɔ:k]	to go on foot (→ A6 walk)	(zu Fuß) gehen
C 1	*simple present* ['sɪmpl 'preznt]		einfache Gegenwart
C 4	for breakfast	I always have coffee ~.	zum Frühstück
C 5	*verb* [vɜ:b]	"to work" is a ~.	Verb, Zeitwort
C 6	**place** [pleɪs]	Can you find a ~ for this picture?	Ort, Platz

1 *on*	a book ~ Scotland	*hier:* über
to find out	Can you ~ what "wages" means? (→ 2/A7 to find)	herausfinden
2 at lunchtime	during the lunch hour (→ 5/D3 lunch)	zur Mittagszeit
3 **big** [bɪg]	Birmingham is a ~ city, over a million people live there. (≠ great → 5/A5)	groß *(räumlich)*
hobby [ˈhɒbɪ]	= *German*	Hobby, Steckenpferd
piano [pɪˈænəʊ]	[!]; = *German;* Can you play "Für Elise" on the ~?	Klavier, Piano
4 **tourist** [ˈtʊərɪst]	[!]; = *German*	Tourist
souvenir [suːvəˈnɪə]	= *German*	Souvenir, Reiseandenken

Unit 7

1 **danger** [ˈdeɪndʒə]		Gefahr
look out!		Vorsicht! Aufpassen!
careful [ˈkeəfʊl]	Be ~ what you say: think before you speak.	vorsichtig
to mind [maɪnd]	M~ the dog. = Careful, there's a dog.	achten auf
head [hed]	You think with your ~.	Kopf
step [step]	Mind the ~s when you leave the house.	Stufe
2 don't [dəʊnt]	= do not; D~ do it!	*(ein Verbot:)* Tu (es) nicht!
to lean [liːn]		lehnen
if [ɪf]	I~ it rains, you must take an umbrella.	wenn, falls
grass [grɑːs]	[!]; = *German*	Gras
3 **home** [həʊm]	the place where you live with your family; house (→ 5/A2 at home, 5/C2 to go home)	Heim, Haus
home finding [ˈfaɪndɪŋ]		auf der Haussuche
to let [let]	This flat is to ~ for £95 per week.	vermieten
to miss [mɪs]	to ~ a bus = to be too late for it (→ 6/A9 missing)	auslassen, verpassen; *hier:* aussetzen
turn [tɜːn]		*hier:* Runde
to miss one turn	All the others can go on, but you can't.	eine Runde aussetzen
to ask [ɑːsk]	He ~s me: "Can you open the window, please?" He ~s me to open the window. (→ 1/D4)	*hier:* bitten
ask him to take you to . . .	(→ 4/B to take)	bitte ihn, dich zu . . . zu bringen
to wait [weɪt]	W~ a minute, I'm coming with you.	warten
too expensive [tuː]	I can't buy it, it's ~.	zu teuer
to move [muːv]	Don't ~, there's a burglar in the bedroom.	(sich) bewegen
to move on		*hier:* ziehen nach . . .
owner [ˈəʊnə]	This is my car. I'm the ~ of the car.	Besitzer, Eigentümer
to give [gɪv]	Can I have a whisky? = G~ me a whisky, please. (give – take)	geben
to give up		aufgeben
4 **to look for**	I'm looking for a coat. Can I get one in this shop?	suchen
a friend of Mr Miller's		ein Freund von Mr Miller
suburb [ˈsʌbɜːb]	Wimbledon is a London ~.	Vorort, Randbezirk

	bus stop [stɒp]	where you get on a bus	Bushaltestelle
	station ['steɪʃn]	where you get on a train	Bahnhof
	supermarket ['su:pəmɑ:kɪt]	[!]; = *German*	Supermarkt
	swimming pool ['swɪmɪŋ pu:l]	In summer I often go to the ~.	Schwimmbad
	to try [traɪ]	I don't think we can do it, but let's ~.	versuchen
	Ask him about where he lives.		Fragen Sie ihn (danach), wo er wohnt.
A 5	**which** [wɪtʃ]	Here are two records: W~ do you like?	welche(r, s)
	beach [bi:tʃ]	On my holiday I like to lie in the sun on the ~.	Strand
	shopping centre ['ʃɒpɪŋ sentə]	where you can buy a lot of things (→ 3/D2 to go shopping)	Einkaufszentrum
A 7	**to stay** [steɪ]	There's a strike today, so I can ~ at home.	bleiben
	to meet [mi:t]	to go to a place and wait for (a friend) (→ 0/1)	*hier:* abholen, treffen
	to take you out	(→ 7/A3 ask him to take you to)	Sie ausführen, mit Ihnen ausgehen
A 8	**music** ['mju:zɪk]	[!]; = *German;* You hear it at a concert.	Musik
	pop music ['pɒp 'mju:zɪk]	[!]; = *German;* modern music: Old people often don't like it.	moderne Schlager
	classical ['klæsɪkl]	*opposite:* modern	klassisch
	art [ɑ:t]	The "Mona Lisa" is a work of ~.	Kunst
	food [fu:d]	the things we eat	Nahrung, Essen
	group [gru:p]	Three people or more are a ~.	Gruppe
A 9	I like listening to music.		Ich höre gern Musik.
	free [fri:]	The tickets are not ~, we have to pay for them.	frei, kostenlos
	free time	time after work	Freizeit
	to enjoy [ɪn'dʒɔɪ]	to like very much (→ 3/A2 to like)	genießen, Freude haben an
	to swim [swɪm]	You can ~ in a swimming pool. (→ A4)	schwimmen
A 10	*interviewer* ['ɪntəvju:ə]	He asks people questions for TV, radio or newspapers.	Interviewer, Befrager
	married ['mærɪd]	They are ~ = they are husband and wife.	verheiratet
	travelling ['trævlɪŋ]	I like ~, I go to Africa or America every year. (→ 6/A10)	Reisen
	pop star ['pɒpstɑ:]	A man or woman who plays pop music.	Popstar, Schlagerstar
	sport [spɔ:t]	= *German*	Sport
A 11	all night		den ganzen Abend, die ganze Nacht
	young [jʌŋ]	*opposite:* old (→ 2/A3)	jung
	to spend [spend] (on)	I like reading. I ~ a lot of money on books.	(Geld) ausgeben (für)
	disco ['dɪskəʊ]		Disko(thek)
A 12	**terrible** ['terəbl]	very bad	furchtbar, schrecklich
	so many [səʊ]		so viele
	drugs [drʌgz]	Heroin and LSD are ~.	Drogen, Rauschgift
	alcohol ['ælkəhɒl]	There is ~ in whisky and wine.	Alkohol
	to agree [ə'gri:]	I ~ = I think so, too.	zustimmen, der gleichen Meinung sein
	What can we do about it? [ə'baʊt]	(→ 2/A6, 2/A7)	Was können wir dagegen tun?
	love [lʌv]		Liebe
	example [ɪg'zɑ:mpl]	"She's reading" is an ~ of the progressive form.	Beispiel

special ['speʃl]	[!]; = *German;* different from the others	spezial, Sonder-
programme ['prəʊgræm]	[!]; = *German;* The TV ~ isn't very good tonight.	Sendung, Programm
phone-in programme	A TV or radio programme where an interviewer talks to people on the phone.	Sendung mit Telefoninterviews
on the radio		im Radio
song [sɒŋ]	"Help" is a famous ~ by the Beatles.	Lied
sort [sɔ:t]	[!]	Sorte, Art
that sort of thing		so etwas
man [mæn]	(→ 1/B)	*hier: kumpelhafte Anrede*
to want [wɒnt]	I ~ a pen ≈ *(höflichere Form:)* I'd like a pen. (→ 3/A13)	wollen, wünschen
to forget [fə'get]	I know him but I always ~ his name.	vergessen
better ['betə]	good - ~ - best (→ 1/A5, 6/A6)	besser
do you want to say		wollen Sie (damit) sagen
Oh come on		Ach, hören Sie auf
person ['pɜ:sn]	Here's a table for 6 ~s. (≈ people → 6/A1)	Person
a person		jemand
a kind of [kaɪnd]	≈ a sort of	eine Art
to believe (in) [bɪ'li:v]	It's a nice story, but I don't ~ it.	glauben (an)
to sing [sɪŋ]	A pop star ~s songs.	singen
to feel [fi:l]	I ~ sorry = I am sorry. See - hear - ~.	(sich) fühlen
important [ɪm'pɔ:tnt]	This piece of news is very ~.	wichtig, bedeutend
show business	TV, pop music, films are all part of ~.	Schaugeschäft, Unterhaltungsbranche
small [smɔ:l]	*opposite:* big (→ 6/D3)	klein
everything ['evrɪθɪŋ]	*opposite:* nothing (→ 4/A10; something 4/A5)	alles
happy ['hæpɪ]		glücklich, froh, zufrieden
to live [lɪv]	(→ 2/A6)	*hier:* leben
all the time	≈ always	die ganze Zeit, immer
girl [gɜ:l]	Jane is a nice ~. (→ 3/C1 girlfriend)	Mädchen
to cross [krɒs]	to go over (the street)	kreuzen, überqueren
to use [ju:z]	You ~ a pen to write a letter.	benutzen, gebrauchen
sentence ['sentəns]	"This is a pen" is a ~.	Satz
manager ['mænɪdʒə]	[!]; = *German*	Manager
to go on	It's late, you can ~ with your work tomorrow.	fortfahren, fortsetzen
text [tekst]	= *German*	Text
to stay up late	to go to bed late (→ 7/A7 to stay; 4/B late)	lange aufbleiben
to show [ʃəʊ]	At the boat show (1/B) they ~ boats, beach clothes, etc.	zeigen

8

Unit 8

hairdresser ['heədresə]	She goes to the ~ every week.	Friseur
to save [seɪv]	*opposite:* to spend	sparen
penny ['penɪ]	1 penny + 1 penny = 2 pence (→ 2/A4)	*hier:* Pfennig
to open	*opposite:* to close (→ 3/B open)	*hier:* eröffnen
one day		eines Tages
so [səʊ]	It's late, ~ I'm going to bed.	daher
full [fʊl]	This bottle is ~ of whisky.	voll

	second-hand	His car is ~. = He is the second (or third, etc.) owner.	aus zweiter Hand, gebraucht, antiquarisch
	second-hand shop	where you can buy old books, clothes, pictures, etc.	Trödler(laden)
	university [ju:nɪ'vɜ:sətɪ]	where students work	Universität
	still [stɪl]	I'm not 21 yet. I'm ~ 20.	noch
	with his parents	(→ 1/B with)	bei seinen Eltern
	who [hu:]	*a thing* which; *a person* ~	der, die, das; welche(r, s)
	centre ['sentə]	(→ 7/A5 shopping ~)	Zentrum, Mittelpunkt
	exam [ɪg'zæm] = **examination** [ɪgzæmɪ'neɪʃn]	[!] You can take an ~ after 2 or 4 years of English at night school.	Examen
	to marry ['mærɪ]	If you ~ a person he/she is then your husband/wife. (→ 7/A10 married)	heiraten
	teacher ['ti:tʃə]	Is your English ~ a man or a lady?	Lehrer(in)
	as [æz]	She works ~ a teacher.	als
	a job as a teacher		eine Stelle als Lehrer
	another [ə'nʌðə]	not the same, one more	ein(e) andere(r, s)
	that is why	= so (→ 0/4 why)	deswegen, daher, deshalb
	out of work	without a job (→ 6/A5 work)	arbeitslos
	waiter ['weɪtə]	He works in a restaurant, bar, etc.	Kellner
	to study ['stʌdɪ]	Students ~ at university.	studieren
	Where do they come from?	(→ 1/A4 Where are you from?)	*hier:* Wo stammen sie her?
A 2	**to get back**	(→ 4/A9 back; 6/A6 to get home)	zurückkommen
A 3	**sure** [ʃʊə]	I'm not ~ = I don't know, but I think . . .	sicher
	do you think?		glauben Sie? glaubst du?
A 4	**to remember** [rɪ'membə]	*opposite:* to forget (→ 7/B)	sich erinnern (an)
	to agree with [ə'gri:]	You're right. I ~ you. (→ 7/A12)	einverstanden sein mit, übereinstimmen mit, zustimmen
	some [sʌm]	a number of, three or more	ein paar, einige
A 6	unhappy [ʌn'hæpɪ]	not happy (→ 7/B)	unglücklich
	late train	a train late at night (→ 4/B late)	Nachtzug
	with all the traffic		bei dem (dichten) Verkehr
	police [pə'li:s]	[!] (→ 5/A9 policeman)	Polizei
A 7	It's a twenty-minute walk.	You have to walk 20 minutes. (→ 6/A6 a walk)	Es sind 20 Minuten zu Fuß.
	different ['dɪfrənt]	*opposite:* same (→ 6/A4)	verschieden
	He has to take three different buses.		Er muß zweimal umsteigen.
	have to	= must	müssen
A 9	**fair** [feə]	= *German*	gerecht
	part [pɑ:t]	Speaking to people on the phone is ~ of my job.	Teil
	part-time job	a job for only 4 or 5 hours a day	Halbtagsstellung, Teilzeitbeschäftigung
	paper ['peɪpə]	= newspaper (→ 6/A1)	(Papier), *hier:* Zeitung
	sports news [spɔ:ts]		Sportnachrichten
	to flirt [flɜ:t]	[!]; = *German*	flirten
	not . . . any more ['enɪ]		nicht mehr
	I really don't think it's fair.		Ich halte das wirklich für (sehr) ungerecht.
	wonderful ['wʌndəfʊl]	great	herrlich, wunderbar

lucky [ˈlʌkɪ]	(≠ happy → 7/B)	glücklich (aus Zufall)
You are lucky.		Du hast Glück.
lots of [lɒts]	= a lot of (→ 1/B, 2/A6)	viel(e), eine Menge
interesting [ˈɪntrəstɪŋ]	Stamps are an ~ hobby.	interessant
much [mʌtʃ]	(→ 2/A4 how much)	viel
safe; safer [seɪf, ˈseɪfə]	It's not ~ to cross the road here.	sicher; sicherer
winter [ˈwɪntə]	*opposite:* summer (→ 5/B)	Winter
life [laɪf]	He lives a quiet ~. (→ 7/B to live)	Leben
My life is just the same.		Mein Leben ist (immer noch) genau das gleiche.
as **before**	(→ 6/A9 before)	wie zuvor
to stop [stɒp]	*opposite:* to start (→ 7/A4 bus stop)	aufhören (mit)
It's their bedtime.	They must go to bed. (→ 6/D2 lunchtime)	Es ist Schlafenszeit für sie.
Love, Jean [lʌv]		*(unter persönlichen, freundschaftlichen Briefen:)* Liebe Grüße, Deine Jean
after all [ɑːftərˈɔːl]		schließlich
After all, what do you do in an office?		Was macht man schließlich im Büro?
all day	(→ 7/A11 all night)	den ganzen Tag
most [məʊst]	a lot of – more – ~	(der, die, das) meiste
most of the time		die meiste Zeit
It's not so much the money.		Es ist nicht so sehr das Geld.
that [ðət]	*a thing* ~/which, (*a person* who/that) (→ 8/A1)	welche(r, s); das, (die, der)
a change [tʃeɪndʒ]	something new or different	Abwechslung, Wechsel, (Ver-)Änderung
to get out of the house	(→ 2/A6 get out of)	aus dem Haus kommen
by the way		übrigens
tired [ˈtaɪəd]	I'm ~. Let's go to bed.	müde
for Eric it's only		für Eric gibt es nur
football [ˈfʊtbɔːl]	I watch ~ on TV every Saturday.	Fußball
It's the same old story.		Es ist (immer) das alte Lied.
away [əˈweɪ]	not at home	weg, fort
love to		Grüße an
loving [ˈlʌvɪŋ]		(Dich) liebende
beginning [bɪˈgɪnɪŋ]	the first part	Anfang
question word	"Where?" and "what?" are question words.	Fragewort
real [ˈrɪəl]	[!]; = *German* (→ 2/A7, 6/B really)	real, wirklich
something **else** [els]		etwas anderes
for example	(→ 7/A12 example)	zum Beispiel
to tell a person what to do		jemandem sagen, was er tun soll
to disagree [dɪsəˈgriː]	*opposite:* to agree (→7/A12)	nicht zustimmen
to think of	(→ 1/B to think)	*hier:* sich ausdenken, finden
any more [ˈenɪ]	(→ A9)	*hier:* weitere
woman [ˈwʊmən]; *pl.* women [ˈwɪmɪn]	(≠ 0/2 wife; ≠ 1/A3 lady; ≠ 1/A5 Mrs; ≠ 4/D2 madam); This job is for men and ~ *(pl.).*	Frau
or me		oder ich
older [ˈəʊldə]	He's 80, and she's even ~. (→ 2/A3 old)	älter
to spend [spend]	How do you ~ your free time? (→ 7/A11 to spend money)	(Zeit) verbringen

	own [əʊn]	I've got my ~ car. = I'm the owner. (→ 7/A3)	eigen
	She doesn't have money of her own.		Sie hat kein eigenes Geld.
	She doesn't feel important.	(→ 7/B to feel)	Sie fühlt sich nicht wichtig.
	as important **as**		so wichtig wie
D 4	**doctor** ['dɒktə]	= *German*	Doktor, Arzt
	at the doctor's	(→ 3/A9 chemist's)	beim Arzt
	hard [hɑ:d]	Housework is ~ work.	hart, schwer
	to sleep [sli:p]	You ~ in your bed.	schlafen
	about 30 cigarettes	27-33 cigarettes	ungefähr 30 Zigaretten
	mile [maɪl]	1 ~ = 1.6 km	Meile
	to take home	(→ 5/A2 at home, 6/A6 get home)	mit nach Hause nehmen

Unit 9

A 1	did [dɪd]	*the simple past of* to do	tat
	yesterday ['jestədɪ]	[!] ~ – today – tomorrow	gestern
	got up	*the simple past of* to get up	stand auf
	ate [et]	[!] *the simple past of* to eat	aß
	left [left]	*the simple past of* to leave	verließ
	took [tʊk]	*the simple past of* to take	nahm
	made [meɪd]	*the simple past of* to make	machte
	had [hæd]	*the simple past of* to have	hatte
	read [red]	[!] *the simple past of* to read	las
	drank [dræŋk]	*the simple past of* to drink	trank
	met [met]	*the simple past of* to meet	traf
	went [went]	*the simple past of* to go	ging
A 3	**camera** ['kæmərə]	[!]; = You take pictures with a ~.	Fotoapparat
	telephone ['telɪfəʊn]	phone (→ 5/A1)	Telefon
	heating ['hi:tɪŋ]	You turn on the central ~ in winter.	Heizung
	hot [hɒt]	It is very ~ in Africa.	heiß
	water ['wɔ:tə]	The swimming pool is full of ~.	Wasser
	inside [ɪn'saɪd]	~ the house = in the house	innerhalb
	was [wɒz]	*the simple past of* to be (I, he, she, it ~)	war
	in 1920		1920
A 4	were [wɜ:]	*the simple past of* to be (You *sg.* + *pl.*, we, they ~)	waren, warst, wart
	told [təʊld]	*the simple past of* to tell (→ 2/A6)	*hier:* sagte, riet, befahl
A 5	**beautiful** ['bju:tɪfʊl]	nice, wonderful, very good	schön
	weather ['weðə]	The ~ is terrible. It's raining.	Wetter
	Have a nice day.		Ich wünsche einen schönen Tag!
A 6	**sunny** ['sʌnɪ]	It's ~, you can see the sun. (→ 5/A6)	sonnig
	cloudy ['klaʊdɪ]	You can't see the sun, it's ~.	bewölkt, wolkig
	cool [ku:l]	Even in summer the nights are often ~.	kühl
	cold [kəʊld]	*opposite:* hot	kalt
	rain [reɪn]	Look at the ~. We must take an umbrella. (→ 4/B to rain)	Regen
	dry [draɪ]	It never rains in California. = It is always ~ there.	trocken
	stormy ['stɔ:mɪ]	This boat is not safe in ~ weather.	stürmisch
	What was the weather like?	(→ 6/A6 like)	Wie war das Wetter?
	Mediterranean [medɪtə'reɪnjən]		Mittelmeer-
	language ['læŋgwɪdʒ]	English and German are ~s.	Sprache

area ['eərɪə]	part of a town, etc.	Gebiet
last [lɑ:st]	~ summer → this summer → next summer	letzte(r, s, n), vorige(r, s, n)
holidays	holiday (→ 5/A6)	Ferien, Urlaub
(two years) **ago** [ə'gəʊ]	I'm 50. Two years ~ I was 48.	vor (zwei Jahren)
spent [spent]	*the simple past of* to spend	verbrachte
lay [leɪ]	*the simple past of* to lie	lag
swam [swæm]	*the simple past of* to swim	schwamm
card [kɑ:d]	Can you play ~s? – Yes, Poker and Bridge.	Karte *(im Kartenspiel)*
tour guide ['tʊə 'gaɪd]	He or she goes sight-seeing with tourist groups.	Reisegruppenleiter, Reiseführer
holiday flat	A flat where you can stay during your holidays.	Ferienwohung
camping ['kæmpɪŋ]	[!]; = *German*	Camping
to go camping	We ~ every summer.	campen, Campingurlaub machen
did you have to?	(→ 8/A7 have to = must)	mußten Sie? mußtest du?
to do the cooking ['kʊkɪŋ]	to make breakfast, lunch and dinner	kochen
to clear up [klɪər'ʌp]	Don't leave your room like that. Clear it up.	aufräumen
had to	*the simple past of* have to (→ 8/A7)	mußte(st), mußten
a busman's holiday ['bʌsmənz]	When a person does his usual, every-day work during the holiday, it's ~ for him.	kein Urlaub vom Alltag
to (be at the airport)		um (am Flughafen) zu(sein)
plane [pleɪn]	If you go to England, you must go by boat or by ~.	Flugzeug
to look forward to ['fɔ:wəd]	I ~ my holidays in Italy.	sich freuen auf
at last	It's 10 o'clock. Where's Linda? – Ah, here she is ~!	endlich
clean [kli:n]	We must do the washing-up. There are no ~ cups.	sauber
had [hæd]	*the simple past of* to have	*hier:* aßen, tranken
under ['ʌndə]	*opposite:* over *or* on	unter
till [tɪl]	from 9 ~ 5 = from 9 to 5	bis
travel agency ['eɪdʒənsɪ]	where you can book a tour or a flight, buy train tickets, etc.	Reisebüro
until [ʌn'tɪl]	= till	bis
spoke [spəʊk]	*the simple past of* to speak	sprach
travel agent ['eɪdʒənt]	He works at the travel agency.	Angestellte(r) im Reisebüro
did not get up at all	(→ 3/A9 Not at all.)	stand überhaupt nicht auf
sweet [swi:t]	Chocolate is ~.	süß
saw [sɔ:]	*the simple past of* to see	sah
to go on like this	(→ 6/A6, 6/B like)	so weitergehen
she had a good time		es hat ihr gut gefallen
a bit [bɪt]	I'm ~ tired = I'm tired, but not very tired.	ein wenig, etwas
at first	at the beginning: A~ I didn't like him, but now I do. (≠ first, then, after that → 3/B)	zuerst, anfangs
pub [pʌb]	where you can have a drink and meet friends	Kneipe, Lokal, Wirtshaus, Wirtschaft
understanding [ʌndə'stændɪŋ]	She is very ~, she tries to understand me. (→ 6/B)	verständnisvoll
funny ['fʌnɪ]	I don't like him; he's ~.	*hier:* komisch, seltsam
She did not like them very much.	(→ 3/A9 Thank you very much)	. . . sehr

9

	she's not very well	(→ 1/B very well)	ihr geht es nicht besonders
	give my **best wishes** to ['wɪʃɪz]	(→ 6/A6: with best wishes)	grüßen Sie . . . herzlich von mir
C 1	*the simple past*	"Went" is the simple past of "to go".	einfache Vergangenheit
	regular form ['regjʊlə fɔ:m]		regelmäßige Form
C 4	irregular form [ɪ'regjʊlə]		unregelmäßige Form
C 5	some more	(→ 8/A4 some)	*hier:* ein paar weitere
D 1	questions on the text		Fragen zum Text
D 2	bought [bɔ:t]	*the simple past of* to buy	kaufte
	I ate only half my breakfast.		Ich aß mein Frühstück nur zur Hälfte.
	sang [sæŋ]	*the simple past of* to sing	sang
	toast [təʊst]	[!]; = *German*	Toast
D 3	**to finish** ['fɪnɪʃ]	≈ to stop (→ 8/B)	beenden
	career [kə'rɪə]	A lot of young people do not know which ~ to take up after school.	Karriere, Laufbahn
	to begin [bɪ'gɪn], began	≈ to start (→ 6/A5; beginning 8/C1)	beginnen
	ex [eks]	= *German*	ehemalige(r, s), Ex-
D 5	as usual ['ju:ʒʊəl]	He was late, ~. He's usually late. (→ 6/A2)	wie üblich, wie gewöhnlich
	drove [drəʊv]	*the simple past of* to drive	fuhr
D 6	following ['fɒləʊɪŋ]	≈ next (→ 3/A3). The ~ Unit is number 10.	folgende(r, s)

Unit 10

A 1	What would you like for breakfast?	(→ 3/A13 I'd like)	Was möchten Sie zum Frühstück?
	any ['enɪ]	Have you got ~ orange juice?	*in Fragen:* (irgend)ein, (irgend)welche(n); *oft auch nicht übersetzt*
	not . . . any	No, we haven't got any.	kein(e, n)
	some [sʌm]	I'd like ~ fruit juice and ~ cornflakes. (→ 8/A4)	etwas, ein paar, einige; *oft auch nicht übersetzt*
	fruit juice ['fru:t 'dʒu:s]	There is no alcohol in ~.	Obstsaft
	cornflakes ['kɔ:nfleɪks]	[!]; = *German*	Cornflakes
	egg [eg]		Ei
	bacon and eggs ['beɪkən]	In Britain they often have ~ for breakfast.	Frühstücksspeck/Schinken mit Ei
	brown [braʊn]		braun
	bread [bred]		Brot
	brown bread		dunkles Brot
	butter ['bʌtə]	= *German*	Butter
	jam [dʒæm]	You usually eat it on white bread.	Marmelade *(sofern nicht aus Orangen oder Zitronen)*
	well [wel]	(→ 1/B very well)	gut *(auf ein Verb bezogen)*
	orange ['ɒrɪndʒ]	= *German*	Orange, Apfelsine
A 2	**menu** ['menju:]	[!] You look at it before you have lunch in a restaurant.	Speisekarte

What would you like to start with?		Womit möchten Sie beginnen?
to follow ['fɒləʊ]	to come after (→ 9/D6 following)	folgen
What would you like to follow?		Was möchten Sie danach?
apple ['æpl]	A~s and oranges are fruit.	Apfel
pear [peə]	[!] P~s are fruit, too.	Birne
sir [sɜ:]	Yes, ~? (→ 4/D2 madam)	mein Herr *(höfliche Anrede, immer ohne Namen gebraucht)*
tomato [tə'mɑ:təʊ]	[!] T~es are red.	Tomate
soup [su:p]	Would you like to start with ~ or fruit juice?	Suppe
chicken ['tʃɪkɪn]	It comes out of an egg.	Küken, Huhn
roast chicken [rəʊst]		Brathähnchen
steak [steɪk]	[!] = *German*	Steak
chips [tʃɪps]	You often eat them with steak.	Pommes frites
to boil [bɔɪl]	to cook (food) in water	kochen, sieden *(Kochen von Eiern, Fisch, Kartoffeln und Gemüse)*
potato [pə'teɪtəʊ]	[!] Germans eat a lot of ~es.	Kartoffel
boiled potatoes		Salzkartoffeln
vegetable ['vedʒtəbl]	In our garden we have flowers and ~s.	Gemüse
salad ['sæləd]	The English often eat chips with fish, not potato ~.	*(angemachter)* Salat
fish [fɪʃ]	We often eat ~ on Fridays.	Fisch
cheese [tʃi:z]	I'd like ice-cream, then ~, and then coffee, please.	Käse
V.A.T. [væt]	value added tax [vælju: 'ædɪd tæks]	Mehrwertsteuer
service ['sɜ:vɪs]	the waiter's work	Bedienung
included [ɪn'klu:dɪd]	You do not have to pay extra for it.	eingeschlossen
luck [lʌk]	I never have any ~. = I'm never lucky. (→ 8/B)	Glück
bad luck	*opposite:* good luck	Pech, Unglück
customer ['kʌstəmə]	person who goes to a shop, restaurant, bank, etc.	Kunde, Kundin, Gast *(im Restaurant)*
instead [ɪn'sted]		stattdessen, dafür
bill [bɪl]	It says how much you have to pay.	Rechnung
change [tʃeɪndʒ]	the money you get back (→ 8/B a change)	Klein-, Wechselgeld
to change [tʃeɪndʒ]	to give money back, e.g. 100p for £1	wechseln
note [nəʊt]	paper money	(Bank-)Note, (Geld-)Schein
cheque [tʃek]	Today people often pay by ~ in department stores etc.	Scheck
cheque card		Scheckkarte
Would you . . . ?		Würden Sie . . . ?
party ['pɑ:tɪ]	= *German*	Party, Gesellschaft
to have a party		eine Party geben
shopping **list**	a piece of paper with the things you want to buy	Einkaufszettel, -liste
No, I'm afraid not.	(→ 1/B I'm afraid)	Nein, leider nicht.
some more	(→ A1 some)	*hier:* noch etwas
beer [bɪə]	Germans drink a lot of ~, Italians drink wine.	Bier
bigger ['bɪgə]	Berlin is big, but London is ~.	größer
bigger **than** [ðæn]	London is ~ Berlin.	größer als
as good **as**	Is Italian wine ~ French wine?	so gut wie

A 8	more expensive	A Rolls-Royce is ~ than a Mini.	teurer
A 9	**map** [mæp]	a ~ of England	(Land-)Karte
	Oxon	= Oxfordshire ['ɒksfədʃə]	*englische Grafschaft*
	private ['praɪvɪt]	[!]; = *German*	privat
	fully licensed ['laɪsənst]	where you can get whisky, beer, etc.	mit Alkoholausschank
	not as good as	I like Italian wine, but it's ~ French wine.	nicht so gut wie
	B & B	bed and breakfast	Übernachtung mit Frühstück
A 10	**best** [best]	good – better – ~	beste(r, s, n)
	most comfortable	comfortable – more comfortable – ~	(am) bequemste(r, s, n)
A 11	private bath	a (hotel) room with ~	eigenes Bad
	extra ['ekstrə]	not included	(wird) gesondert (berechnet)
A 12	the restaurant he is talking about		das Restaurant, über das er spricht
A 13	**lift** [lɪft]	= *German*	Fahrstuhl, Lift
	building ['bɪldɪŋ]	Houses, blocks of flats, towers, factories etc. are ~s.	Gebäude
	to stop [stɒp]	*opposite:* to start (→ 7/A4 bus stop; 8/B to stop)	*hier:* (an-)halten
	also ['ɔ:lsəʊ]	It ~ stops here. = It stops here, too.	auch
	snack-bar ['snækbɑ:]	where you can have a drink or eat when you are in a hurry	Schnellimbiß
	upstairs [ʌp'steəz]	When you go from the first to the second floor, you go ~.	nach oben
	downstairs [daʊn'steəz]	*opposite:* upstairs	nach unten
B	eating out	to have lunch or dinner in a restaurant	essen gehen
	just [dʒʌst]	≈ only; (≠ 5/A4, ≠ 6/B)	*hier:* nur
	meal [mi:l]	breakfast, lunch, dinner = ~s	Mahlzeit, Essen
	easy ['i:zɪ]	*opposite:* difficult (→ 2/A7)	leicht
	for example	(→ 7/A12 example)	zum Beispiel
	less expensive	*opposite:* more expensive (→ 6/B less)	billiger
	international [ɪntə'næʃənl]	[!]; = *German*	international
	wherever [weər'evə]	at or to all places	überall wo, wo auch immer
	world [wɜ:ld]	Tokyo and New York are the biggest cities in the ~.	Welt, Erde
	hamburger ['hæmbɜ:gə]	[!]; Americans like MacDonald's ~s	Brötchen mit Hackfleischsteak
	cheeseburger ['tʃi:zbɜ:gə]	[!]; a hamburger with a piece of cheese in it	Hamburger mit Käsescheibe
	the City ['sɪtɪ]	a part of London, the centre of banks and business	die City
	self-service [self'sɜ:vɪs]	without a waiter (→ A2 service)	Selbstbedienung
	delicacy ['delɪkəsɪ]	something good to eat	Delikatesse
	although [ɔ:l'ðəʊ]	[!] I'm not tired, ~ it's late.	obwohl, obgleich
	foreigner ['fɒrɪnə]	Italians are ~s in Germany.	Ausländer(in)
	alcoholic [ælkə'hɒlɪk]	with alcohol	alkoholisch
	sandwich ['sænwɪdʒ]	[!] You need two pieces of bread, some butter and some cheese to make a cheese ~.	Sandwich
	more and more	(→ 4/B more)	immer mehr
	to offer ['ɒfə]	They ~ed me 3,000 marks for my second-hand car.	(an)bieten
	to get	The food is getting cold.	*hier:* werden

reason ['ri:zn]	Why did you do that? What were your ~s?	Grund
Commonwealth ['kɒmənwelθ]		*Staatenbund Großbritanniens mit den ehemaligen Kolonien*
country ['kʌntrɪ]	England and Germany are countries.	Land
the British ['brɪtɪʃ]	people from Britain (→ 3/A2 British)	die Briten
typical ['tɪpɪkl]		typisch
for some time	(A1 some)	einige Zeit (lang)
I haven't got any time		ich habe keine Zeit
everybody ['evrɪbɒdɪ]	everyone (→ 6/B)	jede(r)
everywhere ['evrɪweə]	(in, at, to) every place	überall (hin)
somebody, someone ['sʌmbədɪ, -wʌn]	a person	jemand
anybody, anyone ['enɪbɒdɪ, -wʌn]	any person	irgend jemand, -eine(r)
anything ['enɪθɪŋ]	(→ something 4/A5; everything 7/B; nothing 4/A10)	irgend etwas
anywhere ['enɪweə]	(in, at, to) any place (→ somewhere 6/B)	irgendwo(hin), überall (hin)
nobody, *no-one* ['nəʊbədɪ, -wʌn]	not anybody, no person	niemand
nowhere ['nəuweə]	not anywhere, (in, at, to) no place	nirgends, nirgendwo(hin)
comparison [kəm'pærɪsn]	"London is bigger than Berlin" is a ~.	Vergleich
short [ʃɔ:t]	(→ 1/C5 short answer)	kurz
long [lɒŋ]	*opposite:* short	lang
for sale [seɪl]	(→ 1/A6 sales manager)	zum Verkauf
salesman ['seɪlzmən]	He tries to sell you something. (→ 1/A6 sales manager)	Vertreter, Verkäufer
sports car	(→ 8/A9 sports news)	Sportwagen
fast [fɑ:st]	A plane is ~er than a bus.	schnell
true [tru:]	≈ right	wahr, richtig
engine ['endʒɪn]	This sports car has got a big ~.	Motor, Maschine
Co-op ['kəʊɒp]		*etwa:* Konsum(laden)
I'd say	(→ 3/A13 I'd like)	ich würde sagen
whiskey ['wɪskɪ]	whisky from Ireland	irischer Whisky
home town	the town where you come from (→7/A3 home)	Heimatstadt

10

Eigennamen

African [ˈæfrɪkən]
Alfred [ˈælfrɪd]
Alison [ˈælɪsn]
America [əˈmerɪkə]
American [əˈmerɪkən]
Andrew [ˈændruː]
Athens [ˈæθɪnz, ˈæθənz]

Barbara [ˈbɑːbərə]
Beech Grove [biːtʃ ˈgrəʊv]
Billingham [ˈbɪlɪŋəm]
Birmingham [ˈbɜːmɪŋəm]
Bonanza [bəˈnænzə]
Bourbon [ˈbɜːbən]
Brighton [ˈbraɪtn]
British [ˈbrɪtɪʃ]
Broughton [ˈbrɔːtn]
Brussels [ˈbrʌslz]

Cairo [ˈkaɪərəʊ]
Calais [ˈkæleɪ]
Canada [ˈkænədə]
Caroline [ˈkærəlaɪn]
Cathy [ˈkæθɪ]
Caversham (Bridge) [ˈkævəʃəmˈbrɪdʒ]
Charles [tʃɑːlz]
Charlie Chaplin [ˈtʃɑːlɪ ˈtʃæplɪn]
Charlotte [ˈʃɑːlət]
Chelsea [ˈtʃelsɪ]
Chester Terrace [ˈtʃestə ˈterəs]
Chinese [tʃaɪˈniːz]
Cologne [kəˈləʊn]

Alex, Colette Dupont [ˈælɪks, kəˈlet d(j)uːˈpɒnt]
Co. (= County) Durham [ˈkaʊntɪ ˈdʌrəm]

Fred Ferguson [fred ˈfɜːgəsn]
France [frɑːns]
French [frentʃ]

George [dʒɔːdʒ]
German [ˈdʒɜːmən]
Germany [ˈdʒɜːmənɪ]
Gledhow Valley Road [ˈgledhəʊ ˈvælɪ ˈrəʊd]
Richard Green [ˈrɪtʃəd ˈgriːn]
Graham Greene [ˈgreɪəm ˈgriːn]

Roger Grey [ˈrɒdʒə greɪ]

Simon Hargreaves [ˈsaɪmən ˈhɑːgriːvz]
Heathrow [ˈhiːθrəʊ]
Henley-on-Thames [ˈhenlɪ ɒn ˈtemz]
Horsley [ˈhɔːzlɪ, ˈhɔːslɪ]
Ralph Howard [rælf ˈhaʊəd]
Hugh [hjuː]
Hull [hʌl]

India [ˈɪndjə]
Ireland [ˈaɪələnd]
Irish [ˈaɪərɪʃ]
Italian [ɪˈtæljən]
Italy [ˈɪtəlɪ]

Jane [dʒeɪn]
Janice [ˈdʒænɪs]
Japan [dʒəˈpæn]
Jean [dʒiːn]

Karen [ˈkærən, ˈkɑːrən]

Littleton & Sons [ˈlɪtltən n ˈsʌnz]
Liverpool Street Station [ˈlɪvəpuːl ˈstriːt ˈsteɪʃn]
London [ˈlʌndən]

Malta [ˈmɔːltə]
Marks and Spencers [ˈmɑːks n ˈspensəz]
St. Mark's [sntˈmɑːks]
Martha [ˈmɑːθə]
Mediterranean [medɪtəˈreɪnjən]
Liza Minelli [ˈlaɪzə mɪˈnelɪ]
Patrick Mulligan [ˈpætrɪk ˈmʌlɪgən]
Munich [ˈmjuːnɪk]

Nigeria [naɪˈdʒɪərɪə]

Onslow Square [ˈɒnzləʊ ˈskweə]
Oostende = Ostend [ɒˈstend]
Oxon. = Oxfordshire [ˈɒksfədʃə]

Pakistani [pɑːkɪˈstɑːnɪ]

Paris [ˈpærɪs]
Perth [pɜːθ]
Portobello Road [pɔːtəʊˈbeləʊ rəʊd]

Regent's Park [ˈriːdʒənts ˈpɑːk]
John Richards & Partners [dʒɒn ˈrɪtʃədz n ˈpɑːtnəz]
Rolling Stones [ˈrəʊlɪŋ stəʊnz]

Selfridges [ˈselfrɪdʒɪz]
Soho [ˈsəʊhəʊ]
South Kensington [saʊθ ˈkenzɪŋtən]
Spain [speɪn]
Swansea [ˈswɒnzɪ]

United States [juːˈnaɪtɪd ˈsteɪts]
Uxbridge [ˈʌksbrɪdʒ]

Valerie [ˈvælərɪ]
Vancouver [vænˈkuːvə]
Venice [ˈvenɪs]
Victoria Station [vɪkˈtɔːrɪə ˈsteɪʃn]
Vienna [vɪˈenə]

Audrey Walker [ˈɔːdrɪ ˈwɔːkə]
Wales [weɪlz]
Watford [ˈwɒtfəd]
Welsh [welʃ]
West Close [ˈwest ˈkləʊs]
West Indies [ˈwest ˈɪndɪz]
Wimbledon [ˈwɪmbldən]

§ 185

Erklärung der Lautschrift

[iː]	langes **i**, etwa wie dt. l**ie**s, n**ie**	l**ea**ve [liːv]
[ɪ]	kurzes **i**, etwa wie dt. S**i**tz	th**i**s [ðɪs]
[e]	kurzes **e**, wie in dt. B**e**tt	p**e**n [pen]
[æ]	offener als **ä** in **ä**hnlich, aber nicht so offen wie **a** in dt. M**a**nn	m**a**n [mæn]
[ə]	kurzes, unbetontes **e**, wie in dt. bitt**e**	**a**gain [əˈgen]
[ɜː]	etwa wie in dt. M**ö**rder, jedoch ohne r-Laut und ohne Lippenrundung	h**er** [hɜː]
[ʌ]	kurzes **a**, weniger offen als **a** in dt. St**a**dt	c**u**p [kʌp]
[ɑː]	langes **a**, etwa wie in dt. V**a**ter, B**ah**n	c**ar** [kɑː]
[ɔː]	langes, offenes **o**, wie in dt. T**o**rf	**al**ways [ˈɔːlweɪz]
[ɒ]	kurzes, offenes **o**, wie in dt. fl**o**tt	n**o**t [nɒt]
[ʊ]	kurzes **u**, etwa wie in dt. P**u**tz	b**oo**k [bʊk]
[uː]	langes **u** mit Lippenrundung, etwas offener als in dt. d**u**, M**u**t	y**ou** [juː]
[aɪ]	etwa wie in dt. f**ei**n	f**i**ne [faɪn]
[eɪ]	etwa von **e** in dt. l**e**sen zu **i** in dt. n**ie** gleitend	n**a**me [neɪm]
[ɔɪ]	etwa wie in dt. Sch**eu**	b**oy** [bɔɪ]
[aʊ]	etwa wie in dt. bl**au**	h**ow** [haʊ]
[əʊ]	etwa von **e** in bitt**e** zu **u** in P**u**tz gleitend	c**oa**t [kəʊt]
[eə]	Einsatz offener als **ä** in dt. B**ä**r zu **e** in bitt**e** gleitend	ch**air** [tʃeə]
[ɪə]	von kurzem **i** wie in dt. S**i**tz zu **e** in bitt**e** gleitend	h**ere** [hɪə]
[w]	wie [uː] mit vorgestülpten Lippen	**w**here [weə]
[v]	ähnlich dt. **W**asser, aber mit den Oberzähnen auf der Unterlippe	**v**ery [ˈverɪ]
[ð]	Zunge an obere Vorderzähne, stimmhaft, weiter vorne im Mund als [z] in dt. **S**ee (‚gelispelt')	**th**e [ðə]
[θ]	Zunge an obere Vorderzähne, stimmlos, weiter vorne im Mund als [s] in **Iß!** (‚gelispelt')	**th**anks [θæŋks]
[s]	wie in dt. wi**ss**en	**s**tamp [stæmp]
[z]	wie in dt. rei**s**en	**z**oo [zuː]
[tʃ]	etwa wie in dt. **Tsch**eche, deu**tsch**	**ch**air [tʃeə]
[dʒ]	etwa wie in dt. **Dsch**ungel, Ada**g**io (stimmhaft)	**j**ob dʒɒb]
[ʃ]	wie in dt. Fi**sch**	**sh**e [ʃiː]
[ʒ]	wie in dt. Gara**g**e, In**g**enieur	televi**s**ion [ˈtelɪvɪʒn]
[r]	der nächste dt. Laut ist [d]; Zunge vom Gaumen leicht zurückbiegen (nicht rollen!)	**r**ight [raɪt]
[ŋ]	wie in dt. la**ng**, ohne [k]-Laut	morni**ng** [ˈmɔːnɪŋ]

Bitte beachten Sie, daß [b], [d] und [g] am Wortende nicht zu [p], [t] bzw. [k] werden dürfen.

Das englische Alphabet

a [eɪ]	b [biː]	c [siː]	d [diː]	e [iː]	f [ef]	g [dʒiː]	h [eɪtʃ]	i [aɪ]
j [dʒeɪ]	k [keɪ]	l [el]	m [em]	n [en]	o [əʊ]	p [piː]	q [kjuː]	r [ɑː]
s [es]	t [tiː]	u [juː]	v [viː]	w [ˈdʌbljuː]	x [eks]	y [waɪ]	z [zed]	

Redewendungen

Wenn Sie den 1. Band von ‚Englisch für Erwachsene B' durchgearbeitet haben, können Sie folgende Sprechabsichten[1] ausdrücken:

1	**Formeln, mit denen man Kontakte anknüpft und sie aufrecht erhält**		
1.1	Jemanden ansprechen und darauf reagieren.	Excuse me. Yes, can I help you?	3/A8-A9
	(am Telefon:)	Hello. Is that Mr Smith? Hello. Can I speak to Mr Smith, please? Yes, speaking. Yes, just a moment. No, I'm afraid he's out.	5/A1-A5, 6/B
1.2	Sich selbst oder jemanden vorstellen und darauf reagieren.	My name is . . . . /I'm . . . . This is . . . . /Meet . . . . Hello. How do you do. How do you do.	0/1-2, 1/A6, 3/A1
1.3	Jemanden grüßen und auf einen Gruß reagieren.	Good morning/afternoon/evening. Good morning/afternoon/ evening. Hello. Hello. Hello. How are you? (I'm) fine, thank you. Very well, thank you. And how are you?	0/1-2, 1/A5-6, 3/A3, 5/A5
1.5	Jemanden verabschieden; sich verabschieden.	Goodbye/'Bye/Bye-bye. Goodbye/. . . . Good night. Good night. Give my best wishes to . . . . Thank you, ...	5/A1, 5/A5, 4/B, 9/B
	(im Brief:)	Yours (sincerely), ...	6/A6, 8/B
1.6	Gute Wünsche aussprechen.	Have a nice day.	9/A5
1.7	Ein Kompliment/Anerkennung aussprechen.	What a nice . . . !/That's a nice . . . . Thanks.	4/A11
1.8	Danken und darauf reagieren.	Thanks/Thanks a lot/Thank you very much. Not at all.	1/A5, 1/B, 3/A8
1.9	Sich entschuldigen.	Sorry.	5/A1

1 Die Begriffe und die Gliederung dieser Zusammenstellung stammen aus dem ‚Grundbaustein Englisch/ VHS-Zertifikat Englisch'. An einigen Stellen folgen sie allerdings einem Verbesserungsvorschlag von Gerda Lauerbach und Jürgen Quetz.

1.10	Jemandem etwas anbieten; auf eine Einladung reagieren.	Would you like a . . . ? Yes, please. That's very kind of you. No, thank you. I'm afraid not.	10/A6, (4/A6)
	(auf eine Bitte hin etwas anbieten/reichen):	(Yes,) here you are	1/B

2	**Wie man ein Gespräch/eine Äußerung einleitet, fortführt und beendet**		
2.1	Ein Gespräch/eine Äußerung einleiten.	Excuse me. Yes, (but) . . . . Look, ... By the way, ... Well, ... Oh no, ...	3/A8, 3/A9 1/B, 2/A7, 2/B 6/B, 7/B 8/B, 9/B 1/B, 2/A7, 2/B 2/A7
2.2	Ein Gespräch/eine Äußerung beenden. (im Brief:)	Right./Alright then. That's all (I wanted to say). I must stop now./That's all for now.	5/A5, 6/B 6/A6, 8/B
2.3	Den Gesprächsablauf sichern; ein Gespräch nicht abreißen lassen; fragen, wenn man etwas nicht verstanden hat.	Pardon? Do you understand? . . . you know	5/A3, 3/B 6/B, 2/B
	(am Telefon:)	I'm sorry, it's a bad line.	5/A3
	(im Unterricht:)	I don't understand. Can you speak more slowly, please? What does 'book' mean? What's 'Buch' in English? How do you pronounce this word? How do you spell 'book'? I see./I don't know. Can I speak German, please?	

3	**Mitteilungen**		
3.1	Etwas benennen, definieren, identifizieren.	It's/That's/This is a . . . . They are . . . . Harris is ICC's sales manager . . . . A train driver is a man who drives trains./A . . . is a thing that is . . . . (I want) this one, (please.)	1/A6, 1/A1, 1/B 3/A1 1/A6 8/A1; 8/B 3/A13
3.2	Etwas begründen.	(Why?) Because of the . . . . because (I can't . . .). That's why . . . . so (her room is . . .). We left at 5 to be in time	0/4 6/B 6/A7 8/A1 8/A1 9/B

4	**Versprechen und Angebote**		
4.1	Anbieten, etwas zu tun.	Can I help you? Yes, please. Thank you, that's very kind of you. No, thank you, it's alright.	4/A6

5 Meinungen

5.1	Ausdrücken, ob man seiner Sache absolut sicher ist, oder ob man seine Aussage mehr oder weniger einschränken möchte.	Of course, ... I'm sure (that) . . . . Perhaps . . . . I think . . . . I'm not sure (that)	2/A7, 4/A10, 4/A12, 4/B, 5/A7, 8/A3, 9/A3-A4, 10/A7-A8
5.2	Auf eine Äußerung eines anderen reagieren (bestätigend, zustimmend, zweifelnd, verneinend, ablehnend, widersprechend).	You're right./That's right. Fine./Alright./Good. I agree it is . . . . Yes, it is/I do/. . . ./it's true. Really? Are you sure? No, it isn't/I don't/. . . . I'm afraid not. I'm afraid I don't agree. I don't think . . . . But . . . ./Oh no, ... I think that's wrong./. . . you're wrong.	0/3, 1/A1, 1/B, 2/A3, 2/A6, 2/A7, 3/B, 4/A2-A3, 4/B, 5/B, 7/A8, 7/A12, 10/A5-A8 etc.

6 Gefühle

6.1	Gefallen/Mißfallen ausdrücken.	I like/enjoy a good cup of tea/swimming. I don't like/enjoy	7/A8, 7/A9, 9/A9
6.3	Ausdrücken, was man tun möchte/haben möchte.	I'd like to go shopping. I'd like a bottle of wine.	3/A3, 5/A5, 10/A1-A3
6.2	Sorge, Hoffnung ausdrücken.	What's the matter? I hope to hear from you	4/A5 6/A6, 8/B
6.6	Zufriedenheit/Unzufriedenheit, Billigung/Mißbilligung ausdrücken.	That's great/fine/good/nice/not bad/terrible.	2/A3, 3/A13, 5/A5, 7/A12 etc.
6.12	Bedauern ausdrücken.	I'm sorry, but I can't help you. I'm afraid I can't help you.	4/A1, 4/A5, 5/A1, 5/D3, 10/A3; 1/B, 9/A3-A4

7 Wie man andere dazu bringt, etwas zu sagen oder zu tun

7.1	Fragen.	(siehe Grammatik-Register)	
7.2	Befehlen, jemanden bitten.	(siehe Grammatik-Register: Imperative)	7/A1-A3
		Can you . . . , please?	4/A5
		Can I have a . . . , please? Yes, of course. Here you are.	10/A3 1/B, 4/A1
7.4	Einen Vorschlag machen.	What about . . . ?/Let's	3/B
7.5	Jemandem einen Rat geben. Jemanden warnen.	Why don't you . . . ? Be careful!/Mind the . . . !	8/A6 7/A1
7.6	Etwas verbieten.	(Please) Don't . . . . You can't	7/A2-A3

Grammatikregister

Alphabetische Wortliste

a, an 1/A4
a week 2/B
about 2/A6, 2/A7, 7/A12; 8/D4
actor 1/A6
address 3/A2
afraid 1/B
after 3/A4
after all 8/B
after that 3/B
afternoon 3/A3
again 1/B
agency 9/B
agent 9/B
ago 9/A8
agree 7/A12, 8/A4
airport 3/A1
alcohol 7/A12
alcoholic 10/B
all 5/B, 7/A11, 7/B, 8/B
alone 6/A3
along 3/A9, 5/A4
already 6/B
alright 3/B
also 10/A13
although 10/B
always 6/A2
a.m. 3/A3
and 0/2
animal 2/B
another 8/A1
answer 1/C5
any 8/A9, 8/D2, 10/A1
anybody 10/C4
any more 8/A9
anyone 10/C4
anything 10/C4
anywhere 10/C4
apple 10/A2
area 9/A7
armchair 2/A2
arr(ival) 4/D6
art 7/A8
as 8/A1, 8/B
as . . . as 8/D3
ask 1/D4, 7/A3
at 1/B, 2/B, 3/A1, 3/A3, 5/A8
at home 5/A2
at last 9/B
at first 9/B
aunt 4/A7
away 8/B

baby-sitter 4/B
back 4/A9
bacon 10/A1
bad 4/A12
bad luck 10/A3
bag 3/B
bank 3/A9
bar 1/B, 4/A9
basement 2/A5
bath 2/A5, 5/D3
bathroom 2/A5
be 1/C4
beach 7/A5
beautiful 9/A5
because 6/A7
because of 6/B
bed 5/D3, 10/A9
bedroom 2/A5
bedtime 8/B
beer 10/A6
before 6/A9
begin 9/D3
beginning 8/C1
believe 7/B
best 6/A6, 10/A10
better 7/B
big 6/D3
bill 10/A3
birthday 4/A8
bit 9/B
block 2/A5
blouse 3/A8
boat 1/B
boil 10/A2
book 0/3
book shop 3/A9
borrow 4/A1
boss 6/B
bottle 5/A6
boyfriend 4/D5
bread 10/A1
break 6/A5
breakfast 6/A4
British 3/A2, 10/B
brother 4/A7
brown 10/A1
building 10/A13
burglar 5/A9
bus 2/A6
business 1/A6
businessman 1/A6
busman 9/B
bus stop 7/A4
but 1/B
butter 10/A1
buy 3/A9
by 2/A6
by the way 8/B
'bye 5/A5
bye-bye 4/B

call 6/A6
camera 9/A3
camping 9/A10
can 1/A5
canteen 6/A6
car 1/A6
card 9/A8
career 9/D3
careful 7/A1
central 2/A5
centre 8/A1
chair 2/A2
change 8/B, 10/A3
cheap 2/A7
cheese 10/A2
cheeseburger 10/B
chemist 3/A9
cheque 10/A3
cheque card 10/A3
chewing-gum 4/A9
chicken 10/A2
child, children 3/A1
chips 10/A2
chocolate 4/A9
Christmas 4/A9
cigarette 1/B
cinema 4/A12
city 1/A4, 10/B
class 2/A6, 3/A4
classical 7/A8
clean 9/B
clear up 9/A10
climb 5/A9
clock 3/A3
close, closed 3/B
clothes 3/A10
cloudy 9/A6
coat 0/4
coffee 6/A6
cold 9/A6
colleague 6/A8
colour TV 2/B
come 4/B, 5/A4, 7/B, 8/A1
comfortable 2/A3
Commonwealth 10/B
comparison 10/C5
concert 4/A9
cooking 9/A10
cool 9/A6
Co-op 10/D4
cornflakes 10/A1
country 10/B
cowboy 5/A5
cross 7/A1
cup 5/A4
customer 10/A3

Dad 4/B
danger 7/A1
daughter 4/A7
day 4/A8
dear 1/B, 4/B, 6/A6
delicacy 10/B
department store 3/A10
dep(arture) 4/D6
desk 2/A2, 3/A10
different 8/A7
difficult 2/A7
dinner 5/A7
disagree 8/C2
disco 7/A11
do 0/2, 3/B, 6/A2
doctor 8/D4
dog 6/A6
door 5/B
downstairs 10/A13
drink 4/B, 5/A4
drive 6/A8
driver 6/A9
drugs 7/A12
dry 9/A6
during 6/A9

early 6/A6
easy 10/B
eat 5/A6
eat out 10/B
egg 10/A1
else 8/C2
engine 10/D2
enjoy 7/A9
enough 4/B
entrance 2/B
even 2/B
evening 1/A5
every 6/A4
everybody 10/C4
everyone 6/B
everything 7/B
everywhere 10/C4
ex 9/D3
exam(ination) 8/A1
example 7/A12, 10/B
excuse 3/A8
expensive 2/A3
extra 10/A11
factory 6/A6
fair 8/A9
family 3/A1
family name 3/A2
famous 5/A6
fast 10/D2
father 4/A7
feel 7/B
fill in 4/D2
film 4/A12
find 2/A7
find out 6/D1
fine 0/2
finish 9/D3
first 1/A5, 3/A8, 3/B, 9/B
first name 1/A5
fish 10/A2
flat 2/A5
flight 3/A7
flirt 8/A9
floor 3/A8
flower 2/A6
follow 10/A2
following 9/D6
food 7/A8
foot, feet 2/A6
football 8/B
for 1/B, 5/A3
foreigner 10/B
forget 7/B
form 9/C1
forward 9/B
free 7/A9
friend 3/B
from 1/A4, 2/A5, 3/B
fruit 10/A1
full 8/A1
fully licensed 10/A9
funny 9/B

garage 2/A5
garden 2/A5
gate 3/A7
get 3/A8, 10/B
get back 8/A2
get home 6/A6
get on 5/A8
get out of 2/A6, 8/B
get to 6/A9
get up 6/A4
girl 7/B
girlfriend 3/C1
give 7/A3
give up 7/A3
glass 5/A7

Bildquellen: Ullstein Bilderdienst, Berlin: Seite 1 (Winston Churchill, Muhammad Ali, Elizabeth Taylor); Camera Press, London: Seite 1 (Charlie Chaplin), Seite 71 (Picket line)

Karten (innere Umschlagseiten): Christa Scheibner, Soltau